Financial Independence for Couples:

Building Wealth Together

ISHAN ROY

Copyright Page

Copyright © 2024 All rights reserved.

No part of this book may be reproduced, stored in a retrieval system, or transmitted in any form or by any means, electronic, mechanical, photocopying, recording, or otherwise, without the prior written permission of the publisher, except for brief quotations used in reviews or scholarly works.

Disclaimer:

The information provided in this book is for educational and informational purposes only and is not intended as financial advice. Readers should consult with a qualified financial advisor before making any financial decisions.

TABLE OF CONTENT

Introduction

For many people, becoming financially independent is a compelling goal, but pursuing it as a partnership can have even more life-changing consequences. In order to assist couples create a bright future together, "Financial Independence for Couples: Building Wealth Together" provides ideas, insights, and useful guidance. It also examines the special dynamics of attaining financial freedom with a spouse.

- **The Idea of Financial Self-Sufficiency**

At its foundation, financial independence is the ability to support oneself comfortably without the need for a regular job. It refers to having enough wealth or passive income to pay your expenses and provide you the flexibility to make decisions based more on your own preferences than your need for money. The goal is to build up a safety net of funds that allows you to focus on your interests, hobbies, or early retirement.

Earning, saving, investing, and prudent money management are often the steps on the route to financial independence. It's about making wise financial decisions, living below your means, and making long-term investments that increase your wealth. However, there are more opportunities and levels of complication when doing this as a couple. When two people collaborate and have similar financial objectives, they can more successfully use one other's assets and abilities to become financially independent.

- **Reasons to Work Towards Financial Independence Together with Your Spouse**

There are several advantages to pursuing financial independence as a marriage that go beyond simply reaching stability. Here are some reasons why it can be quite beneficial to collaborate on this journey:

1. Common Objectives and Vision: Couples who start the journey towards financial freedom jointly build a common future vision. This common objective ensures that both partners are involved in the same financial goals and encourages teamwork and commitment. By coordinating their financial decisions with their long-term goals, it fortifies their partnership as they strive towards a shared goal.

2. Enhanced Financial Management: Better financial results might arise from combining finances and managing money together. Couples that combine their wealth can take advantage of better prices, economies of scale, and investment opportunities that might not be available to them alone. An approach to budgeting, saving, and investing that is more thorough is made possible by joint financial management.

3. Social Assistance: Achieving financial independence can be a difficult and frustrating process. Having a companion with whom to experience highs and lows offers emotional support and motivation. Couples are able to celebrate victories, overcome financial obstacles together, and maintain motivation in the face of obstacles.

4. Joint Accountabilities: Budgeting, managing costs, and investment planning are just a few of the many duties involved in financial management. When a couple collaborates, they can assign these tasks according to each other's preferences and individual strengths. The efficient and effective coverage of all facets of financial management is ensured by this division of labour.

5. Enhanced Responsibility: A structure of accountability is established when a couple strives for financial independence. It is the joint responsibility of both spouses to maintain financial goals of course, make wise judgements, and encourage each other's sound financial practices. Accountability can assist in avoiding financial mistakes and encourage prudent investment and saving practices.

- **The Significance of Interaction**

Any successful partnership is built on effective communication, which is especially important when it comes to money management. To lay a strong foundation for their financial journey, couples need to be honest about their financial principles, habits, and ambitions. This comprises:

- **Building Objectives:** Establishing precise short- and long-term financial goals contributes to the alignment of the two parties. Having shared goals gives direction and focus to any endeavour, be it emergency fund building, retirement planning, or saving for a down payment on a home.

- **Talking About Values:** It's critical that you comprehend one another's priorities and financial values. While some partners might put more of an emphasis on saving for trips, others might be more interested in real estate investing. A harmonious financial plan that honours the goals of both partners can be created by bringing these principles into alignment.

- **Resolving Conflicts:** Debates about money are frequent, but they can be resolved by polite, honest communication. Couples can resolve problems amicably and come to well-informed conclusions by talking about differences in viewpoints and identifying points of agreement.

- **Assembling the Conditions for Achievement**

This book's realistic tactics and doable recommendations are intended to assist couples in reaching financial independence. Important subjects including controlling debt, accumulating wealth, integrating finances, and tax planning are covered. Every chapter provides information on a different facet of money management, with an emphasis on how couples can cooperate to reach their financial objectives.

Achieving financial independence involves meticulous preparation, dedication, and cooperation. Couples can create a stable financial future and take advantage of more freedom and flexibility by comprehending and putting the concepts of financial independence into practice within the framework of their partnership.

- **What to Expect**

In the following chapters, readers will delve into important subjects like:

- Combining Finances: How to identify financial roles and duties, set collaborative budgets, and integrate or manage finances successfully.

- Building Wealth Together: Techniques for planning, saving, and investing in order to reach significant financial objectives, such as homeownership and retirement.

- **Managing Debt:** Strategies for debt repayment, debt avoidance, and emergency fund accumulation.

- **Tax Planning and Optimisation:** Advice on how to file taxes jointly, comprehend couple's tax advantages, and choose investments that minimise taxes.

- **Navigating Financial Challenges:** Techniques for resolving conflicts, organising significant life events, and getting expert counsel.

- **Maintaining Financial Harmony:** Strategies for encouraging candid conversations, acknowledging financial achievements, and making adjustments for changing objectives.

Couples can improve their financial literacy, fortify their relationship, and get one step closer to financial independence by heeding the advice in this book.

Though the path may be difficult, couples can create a safe and bright future together if they work hard and work together.

Chapter One

Setting the Base Foundation

It takes a solid foundation based on open communication, mutual understanding, and well defined goals for a couple to become financially independent. Creating this groundwork is essential to negotiating the challenges of collaborative financial management and cooperating to accomplish your financial goals. This section will examine the essential components of building a strong financial foundation for couples, including knowing each partner's financial history, discussing financial goals, and developing a shared financial vision.

- **Explaining Financial Objectives**

Any successful partnership is built on effective communication, and this is particularly true when it comes to money management. It is ensured that both couples are striving towards the same objective and are in agreement when there is open and honest conversation about financial goals. Here's how to tackle this crucial element:

1. Start Off with Open Discussions: Start by being open and honest with each other about your respective and combined financial objectives. This covers both immediate ambitions like buying a new appliance or saving for a trip, as well as long-term ones like buying a house or making retirement plans. Both partners have a better understanding of each other's priorities and motives by discussing these goals.

2. Set Priorities in Order: It is not uncommon for partners to prioritise different finances. For instance, one spouse might put more emphasis on funding a child's education than the other, with the latter concentrating on retirement investments. Compromising and working together are necessary to align these priorities. Find ways to take into account the priorities of both spouses and talk about how each goal fits into your overall financial plan.

3. Set SMART Goals: Use the SMART criteria (Specific, Measurable, Achievable, Relevant, and Time-bound) to help you reach your financial goals more easily. For example, establish a precise target like "save $10,000 for a down payment on a house within the next two years" rather than a general one like "save more money." There is direction and clarity with this approach.

4. Consistent Visits: Financial objectives should be periodically reviewed and revised. Plan recurring check-ins to assess your progress, make any necessary goal adjustments, and discuss any changes to your financial circumstances. These check-ins guarantee that you remain in sync and are able to adjust to any changing conditions or opportunities.

- **Forging a Common Financial Goal**

For your couple's financial decisions and actions to be guided, you both need to have the same financial vision. Together, you must create a clear vision for your financial future and establish a plan of action to get there. This is how to establish a common financial vision:

1. Define Your Financial Future: Talk about and agree upon what it means for you both to be financially independent. This could involve goals like having several properties, seeing the world, or retiring early.

You can cooperate to bring each other's visions to life by getting to know one another's goals.

2. Create a financial strategy: Make a thorough financial plan that details the steps you will take to realise your common goal. Budgeting, saving, investing, and debt management techniques should all be part of this plan. Divide your long-term objectives into manageable steps, and set benchmarks to monitor your advancement.

3. Establish Financial Values: Decide upon and commit to your basic financial principles, such as thrift, altruism, or stability of finances. These principles will direct your financial choices and assist you in adhering to your vision in the face of difficulties.

4. Make a financial schedule: Create a financial calendar with the dates and deadlines that are significant to your financial objectives. This could include annual financial planning sessions, investment evaluations, and bill due dates. A financial calendar guarantees that important deadlines are met and keeps you organised.

- **Knowing the Financial History of Each Partner**

Knowing each partner's financial history, including their assets, debts, income, and spending patterns, is crucial for laying a solid financial foundation. You can avoid any disputes and make well-informed judgements with the help of this knowledge. Here's how to tackle this part:

1. Exchange Financial Backgrounds: Talk about your personal financial histories, including past financial struggles, routines, and experiences. This includes disclosing details regarding any assets, liabilities, and sources of income. Mutual understanding of one another's financial history promotes openness and confidence.

2. Evaluate Your Financial Assets and Liabilities: Determine the financial advantages and disadvantages of each partner. While one partner might be good at investing, the other might be the better budgeter. Acknowledging these advantages enables you to efficiently distribute financial duties and capitalise on each other's proficiency.

3. Examine your credit report: To learn about each other's credit histories, get and examine your credit reports. This can give you a baseline for raising your credit ratings and assist in identifying any possible problems. Having a solid credit history is essential for getting loans and reaching financial objectives.

4. Talk About Financial Expectations: Share your goals for your lifestyle and money management. This covers your strategies for managing regular spending, large expenditures, and unexpected financial obligations. By matching these expectations, it is possible to avoid misunderstandings and make sure that both parties are in agreement.

- **Installing Financial Mechanisms**

After you've built a solid foundation, it's critical to put procedures and systems in place for efficient money management. This comprises:

1. Assembling a Collective Budget: Create a shared budget that details your combined income, out-of-pocket costs, and savings objectives. A combined budget lets you manage your money more effectively and gives you a clear view of your financial status.

2. Creating Joint Accounts: For pooled savings and spending, think about opening joint accounts. This can guarantee that both parties contribute to shared objectives and streamline financial management. Don't forget to talk about how costs will be split and how much each partner will contribute.

3. Scheduling Payments and Savings: To make sure you maintain your financial goals, automate bill payments and saves. Schedule automated payments for recurring invoices and set up automatic transfers to savings accounts. Automation lowers the possibility of late payments and promotes budgetary restraint.

4. Creating Financial Barriers: Establish financial checkpoints to assess your progress and make any necessary adjustments to your plan. These checkpoints could be evaluations of your savings, investments, and budget that happen on a weekly, quarterly, or annual basis.

Creating a strong base is the first step to become financially independent as a pair. You may establish a solid partnership that supports your financial objectives by having excellent communication, coming up with a common financial vision, and being aware of each other's financial experiences. You may effectively and consistently manage your funds by putting in place clear protocols and procedures. You and your spouse can boldly start your journey to financial independence with a solid foundation in place, cooperating to realise your goals and ensure a profitable future.

➢ Expressing Financial Objectives

One of the most important factors in reaching financial freedom as a marriage is effective communication about financial objectives. It is easier to make sure that both spouses are on the same page, aware of each other's priorities, and dedicated to a common financial goal when there is open and honest communication about money. This section explores methods for overcoming disagreements, starting and sustaining fruitful discussions about financial objectives, and encouraging a team-based approach to financial planning.

- **Starting Honest Discussions**

Establishing a solid foundation requires having the difficult but necessary conversation about financial objectives. Here's how to handle this important conversation:

1. Select the Appropriate Time: Choose a quiet, impartial moment to talk about money problems. Avert stressful or contentious moments. It can be beneficial for both partners to focus and participate positively if specific time is set up for these talks.

2. Act with Integrity and Openness: Be upfront and honest about your financial dreams, worries, and goals. Being truthful fosters trust and helps prevent misunderstandings. Give a thorough explanation of your present financial circumstances, including your income, assets, obligations, and spending patterns.

3. Create an Agenda: Organise the discussion to cover important subjects in a methodical manner. Talking about immediate objectives, like saving for a trip, medium-term goals, like purchasing a house, and long-term goals, like retirement planning, could fall under this category. An agenda helps to maintain the focus and productivity of the conversation.

4. Listen Actively: Pay attention to your partner's objectives and worries. Be understanding and compassionate, and refrain from interjecting. In order to create a cooperative financial plan, active listening is essential for making both partners feel heard and appreciated.

- **Scheduling Objectives**

Partners may have divergent objectives and viewpoints when it comes to money. Setting these priorities in line requires negotiation and compromise:

1. Identify Common Goals: Begin by determining goals that both couples are enthusiastic about and that are shared. This could be a common goal that both of them have, like travelling or purchasing a home, which can inspire them both.

2. Talk About Competing Priorities: Take up any issues that need attention and figure out how to strike a balance. For example, if one couple prioritises early retirement while the other wants to save more for a child's education, talk about how to combine both goals into your financial plan.

3. Agree to Bargain: Be ready to compromise and look for a middle ground. This could entail redistributing resources or changing deadlines. To create a financial plan that both parties are happy with, compromise is essential.

4. Set Shared Goals: Decide on quantifiable, precise objectives that take into account the priorities of both spouses. For instance, establish a shared objective like "save $15,000 for a down payment on a house within two years" rather than concentrating on individual goals. Goals that are mutually understood promote dedication and teamwork.

- **Creating SMART Objectives**

Your financial objectives might be more specific and actionable if you use the SMART criteria, which stand for Specific, Measurable, Achievable, Relevant, and Time-bound:

1. Specific: Clearly state your objectives. Rather than just aiming to "save more money," be more specific about how much you want to save and why. Say, "Set aside $5,000 for a trip to Europe."

2. Measurable: To monitor your progress, make sure your objectives are quantifiable. Establish monetary goals and benchmarks. For instance, "achieve a total of $5,000 by saving $500 per month for the next ten months."

3. Achievable: Establish reachable, realistic goals in light of your financial circumstances. When you make goals, take your income, spending, and amount of savings into account. Steer clear of too ambitious or unrealistic aspirations.

4. Important: Match your objectives to your priorities and overarching financial vision. Make sure the objectives you set are important to both spouses and contribute to your long-term financial goals.

5. Time-bound: Set a precise deadline for accomplishing your objectives. Say, "Save $2,000 for an emergency fund within six months," as an example. A deadline keeps one motivated and focused.

- **Consistent Visits**

Maintaining your financial objectives and adjusting to changes in your circumstances require frequent check-ins:

1. Arrange for Periodic Reviews: Decide on regular timeframes (such as monthly or quarterly) for reviewing your financial development. Utilise these check-ins to evaluate your progress towards your objectives, spot any roadblocks, and make the required corrections.

2. Celebrate Milestones: Note and honour significant junctures and accomplishments along the path.

Honouring accomplishments keeps you motivated and emphasises how important it is to collaborate to reach your objectives.

3. Modify Objectives as Required: Be adaptable and prepared to modify your objectives in light of shifting priorities or financial circumstances. You might need to adjust your goals and strategy due to unforeseen expenses or changes in your work or personal circumstances.

4. Promptly Address Issues: Deal with any problems or disputes as soon as you come across them. Clear and honest communication facilitates conflict resolution and maintains the direction of the financial planning process.

- **Encouraging a Team Environment**

Developing a cooperative approach to financial planning entails supporting and cooperating on one another's financial objectives:

1. Assign Accountabilities: Depending on the interests and strengths of each partner, divide the financial duties. For instance, one spouse may be in charge of budgeting and the other of investing plans. It is ensured that both partners actively participate in the financial planning process when duties are shared.

2. Support Each Other: Encourage and assist one another in achieving their financial objectives. When assistance is needed, provide it, and cooperate to overcome obstacles. Working together improves your relationship and makes it easier for you to become financially independent.

3. Promote Continuous Communication: Maintain open and continuous channels of communication. Talk about any modifications to your strategy, new objectives, or changes in your financial status on a regular basis. Ongoing communication keeps everyone in sync and guarantees that both parties are informed and involved.

4. Consult a Professional: Seek help and direction from specialists or financial consultants as needed. Expert advice can offer insightful information and support you in making well-informed judgements on your financial objectives and tactics.

Achieving financial freedom as a marriage requires efficient communication of financial goals. A solid foundation for shared financial success can be established by couples through regular check-ins, SMART goal setting, priority alignment, and open communication. Encouraging cooperation and supporting one another's ambitions strengthens the relationship and raises the possibility of achieving common financial goals. Couples can successfully manage their financial journey together and attain long-term financial independence with open communication and shared commitment.

➢ Formulating a Mutual Financial Goal

For couples hoping to become financially independent together, developing a shared financial vision is crucial. A shared vision unites the values, ambitions, and objectives of both parties, offering a direct route to long-term financial success. This section will look at the process of creating a shared financial vision, how to keep it updated, and how to modify it over time.

- **Establishing Fundamental Principles and Goals**

Understanding and coordinating your basic beliefs and financial goals is the first step towards creating a unified financial vision:

1. Identify Core Values: Talk about and determine your fundamental beliefs around money. Values could include being financially secure, being independent, giving back, or having fun. A financial plan that appeals to both partners is shaped in part by an understanding of their respective beliefs.

2. Agree on Common Goals: Set agreed values-based financial goals together. Goals could be buying a house, putting money down for retirement, paying for school, or taking trips. Make sure that the priorities and wishes of both partners are reflected in these goals.

3. Order Objectives: After you've determined what your goals are, order them according to priority and deadline. This will assist you in making strategic decisions that forward your vision and in allocating resources in an efficient manner.

- **Vision Statement Creation**

Your long-term financial goals are expressed in your vision statement, which also acts as a framework for decision-making:

1. Write a Vision Statement. Create a vision statement together that encapsulates your common financial objectives and aspirations. For instance, "We want to become financially independent so that we can travel the world, retire at a comfortable age of 55, and fund our children's education."

2. Make it Inspiring: Make sure the words in your vision statement inspire and motivate others. It should give you a sense of direction and purpose by reflecting your goals and desires.

3. Examine and Improve: As your circumstances and objectives change, revisit and improve your vision statement on a regular basis. Having a changing vision makes your financial planning more current and flexible.

- **Creating a Plan of Action**

The actions and tactics necessary to realise your common financial objective are outlined in a strategic plan:

1. Establish both short- and long-term objectives: Divide your vision into manageable short- and long-term objectives. Long-term objectives could include saving for retirement or real estate investment, while short-term objectives might be setting up an emergency fund or paying off debt.

2. Create a Budget: Make sure your detailed spending plan is in line with your financial objectives. Add your earnings, outgoings, investments, and savings. A well-organised budget makes it easier to monitor your progress towards your goal.

3. Develop an investing Strategy: Make an investing plan that will help you achieve your long-term objectives. Investing in stocks, bonds, property, or other assets could fall under this category. When creating your plan, take your time horizon, investing objectives, and risk tolerance into account.

4. Make a Plan for Savings: Make a savings plan that specifies the amount you must save on a regular basis in order to reach your objectives. Timelines and precise savings goals must be part of this strategy.

5. Debt Management Strategy: If you are in debt, create a plan to control and pay it off. To ease financial burden, give priority to high-interest obligations and take into account options like debt consolidation or refinancing.

- **Keeping Your Vision Sharp and Modifying It**

It's critical to hold onto and modify your financial vision as your objectives and circumstances change in life:

1. Continually Evaluate Your Development: Plan frequent evaluations to evaluate your advancement towards your objectives. Examine your budget, monitor your investments and savings, and analyse financial statements. Make the required changes and stay on course with the help of these reviews.

2. Communicate Changes: Inform each other of any modifications to your financial situation or objectives. Maintaining open lines of communication makes sure that both parties are aware of changes and can work together to resolve any problems.

3. Adapt to Life Changes: Events in your life that affect your financial goals include marriage, having children, changing careers, and making significant purchases. Be ready to realign your goals and modify your plan as necessary to account for these developments.

4. Acknowledgement of Success: Honour your progress and accomplishments along the road. Acknowledge and honour your accomplishments to keep yourself motivated and to reaffirm your dedication to the common goal.

- **Developing Robust Financial Practices**

The effective execution of your shared financial vision is facilitated by sound financial habits:

1. Exercise Discipline: Follow your investing strategy, savings plan, and budget. In order to achieve long-term goals and preserve financial stability, one must practise financial discipline.

2. Promote Accountability: Take responsibility for one another's financial choices and deeds. Ensuring that both parties are contributing to and remaining dedicated to the common vision is facilitated by frequent check-ins and open communication.

3. Educate Yourself: Keep learning about investing and personal money techniques. Possessing knowledge enables you to adjust to shifting financial circumstances and make wise judgements.

4. Seek Professional Guidance: If you're looking for expert guidance, think about speaking with financial advisors or other specialists. Expert advice can offer insightful advice and support as you make difficult financial decisions.

- **Encouraging a Team Environment**

A cooperative approach to financial planning improves your potential to realise your common goal and fortifies your partnership:

1. Assign Accountabilities: Depending on the interests and strengths of each partner, divide the financial duties. For instance, one partner may be in charge of investing and the other of budgeting. Joint responsibility guarantees both partners' active participation.

2. Support Each Other's Goals: Encourage and assist one another in achieving both personal and group financial objectives. Collaboration and mutual assistance build a sense of dedication and collaboration.

3. Maintain Flexibility: Remain willing to modify your goals and financial plan as circumstances dictate. Being flexible enables you to stay in line with your objectives while adjusting to new conditions.

4. Celebrate Successes Together: Come together to recognise and commemorate victories and significant anniversaries. Rejoicing in accomplishments fortifies your relationship and reaffirms your dedication to the common goal.

The first step towards becoming financially independent as a partnership is developing a shared financial vision. Couples can lay a strong foundation for financial success by defining their basic beliefs, establishing shared goals, creating a vision statement, and creating a strategic plan.

A collaborative approach, good financial habits, and vision maintenance and adaptation all increase the chances of achieving long-term financial goals. Couples can work together to accomplish long-term financial independence and realise their financial goals by being transparent with one another, showing support for one another, and making a commitment.

➢ Recognising the Financial History of Each Partner

Establishing a strong basis for your partnership's financial independence requires you to be aware of each partner's financial history. Investigating each person's unique financial background, spending patterns, and mindsets is part of this process. Through acquiring knowledge about each partner's financial history and current situation, couples can enhance goal alignment, tackle possible obstacles, and establish a cohesive financial management strategy.

- **Evaluating Financial Backgrounds**

1. Examine Financial History: Exchange and go over each other's financial backgrounds first. Talk about prior financial experiences, such as schooling, earnings from a career, important financial choices, and prior financial difficulties. Knowing these stories puts each partner's present financial status and attitudes in perspective.

2. Examine Previous Financial Difficulties: Talk about any previous financial setbacks, like debt, bankruptcies, or bad credit. Recognising these difficulties makes it easier to spot possible problem areas and create solutions. Additionally, it promotes compassion and cooperation.

3. List Your Financial Accomplishments: Emphasise any financial accomplishments, such as paying off debt, investing sensibly, or setting aside money for a big purchase. Acknowledging these successes can boost self-esteem and lay the groundwork for future financial planning.

- **Assessing Present Financial Situation**

1. Distribute Financial Records: Important financial documents, such as bank statements, investment accounts, credit reports, and insurance policies, should be exchanged and reviewed. This openness guarantees that each partner is informed of the other's financial situation as of right now.

2. Talk About Revenue and Outlays: Give a thorough rundown of your normal spending and sources of money today. A realistic budget and aligned financial goals are made possible by having a mutual understanding of each other's money inflows and expenditures.

3. Evaluate Debt and Obligations: Examine any outstanding bills, including credit card balances, mortgages, personal loans, and student loans. Evaluating debt levels is essential to creating a plan for managing debt and setting payback priorities.

4. Assess Savings and Assets: Determine what assets you have, such as retirement funds, real estate, savings accounts, and other investments. Knowing each partner's assets facilitates the creation of a thorough financial strategy and the setting of reasonable financial objectives.

- An Examination of Financial Attitudes and Habits

1. Talk About Spending patterns: Provide details about your spending patterns, including how you handle savings, budgeting, and discretionary spending. Recognising possible problems and areas for development is made easier by being aware of each partner's spending patterns.

2. Recognise Your Preferences for Investing and Saving: Talk about the ways you invest and save. For instance, one partner might be more aggressive when it comes to investing, while the other might favour caution. Getting these preferences in line facilitates the creation of a coherent investing plan.

3. Examine Perceptions Regarding Finances: Examine the perspectives that each couple has towards money, particularly their views on risk, wealth, and financial stability. Comprehending these mindsets facilitates the resolution of possible disputes and harmonises monetary objectives with mutual principles.

4. Talk About Your Financial Aspirations and Goals: Talk about your personal financial objectives and desires, such as house ownership, business startup, or early retirement. Prioritising financial goals and developing a cohesive vision are made easier when everyone is aware of one other's aspirations.

- **Aligning Values with Financial Goals**

1. Set Shared Budgetary Objectives: Determine shared financial objectives that complement each partner's values and aspirations based on your discussions. Establishing shared objectives promotes dedication and teamwork.

2. Set priorities for your goals and objectives: Sort your financial objectives according to priority and deadline. Choose which objectives to prioritise and design a strategy to reach them. Setting priorities aids in maintaining focus and efficient resource allocation.

3. Create a Common Financial Vision: Create a financial vision that is a reflection of your shared values and objectives. Your financial decisions and plans are guided by a clear vision that gives you direction and inspiration.

4. Create a Unified Budget: Prepare a budget that accounts for the earnings, outlays, savings, and contributions from investments for both partners. You may successfully manage your funds by ensuring accountability and transparency with a single budget.

- **Resolving Conflicts Regarding Finances**

1. Open Communication: Encourage frank and transparent dialogue around financial issues. Constructively resolve any conflicts or issues by putting more emphasis on finding answers than assigning blame.

2. Seek Compromise: Be prepared to make concessions when it comes to budgetary choices and tactics.

Achieving common financial objectives and preserving harmony require adaptability and flexibility.

3. Determine Accountable Positions and Accountabilities: Specify the duties and responsibilities of each partner in terms of money management. For instance, one partner might be in charge of budgeting and the other of investing. Roles that are clearly defined simplify and prevent confusion in financial management.

4. Take Into Account Financial Counselling: If problems with money don't go away, think about consulting a financial expert or counsellor. Expert support can offer unbiased perspectives and encourage fruitful dialogues.

- **Forging a Robust Financial Alliance**

1. Encourage reciprocal assistance: Encourage one another's financial decisions and aspirations. Promote responsible financial practices and share in accomplishments.

2. Preserve Transparency: Inform one another about important financial choices, adjustments to income, and big outlays. Being transparent guarantees that all parties are on the same page and fosters trust.

3. Continually Review and Adjust: Make sure your goals and financial plan are still relevant and attainable by reviewing them on a regular basis. As priorities or conditions change, make the necessary adjustments to your strategies.

4. Dedication to Ongoing Enhancement: Always look for methods to make your financial planning and management better. Keep yourself updated on the latest tactics and trends in personal finance, and be willing to change and grow.

Establishing a solid basis for financial independence as a partnership requires an understanding of each partner's financial history. Couples can create a cohesive financial management strategy by analysing past financial performance, assessing present circumstances, examining behaviours and attitudes, and coordinating objectives.

Resolving disputes, encouraging cooperation, and upholding openness all help to improve the financial relationship. Couples can work together to accomplish their financial goals and create a secure financial future by being upfront with each other and showing commitment to the process.

Chapter Two

Combining Finances: A Thorough Method for Partners

A big step towards creating a shared financial future for a couple is combining their money. Combining your finances demands careful planning, honest communication, and a clear grasp of each partner's financial habits and objectives—whether you're getting married, starting a family, or just trying to simplify financial management. Managing common spending and financial objectives, as well as integrating financial records and draughting a collaborative budget, are all part of this procedure.

- **Evaluating the Requirement for Merging Financials**

1. Assessing the Stage of Your Relationship: The stage of a relationship typically influences the choice to merge funds. It might make sense for married or soon-to-be married couples to combine their finances. However, combining funds may call for more thought and consent from both parties in less formal unions.

2. Comprehending the Advantages and Disadvantages of Finance: A united approach to budgeting, common financial goals, and easier financial administration are just a few advantages of combining funds. It does have some possible disadvantages, though, like handling debt or having contradictory spending habits. Having a thorough understanding of these elements aids in decision-making.

- **Categories of Financial Contracts**

1. Combined Accounts: Combining finances often involves opening joint bank accounts. Both partners can make deposits and withdrawals, handle spending, and keep tabs on expenditures using joint accounts. They help with collaborative financial management, but openness and trust are necessary.

2. Different Accounts with Complimentary Charges: Some couples use a joint account for shared costs but choose to keep their individual accounts separate. This setup gives each person their own financial independence while offering a centralised method of handling shared expenses like rent, utilities, and groceries.

3. Complete Integration of Finances: Integrating all assets and financial accounts into a single financial system is known as full integration. This method guarantees that all income, expenses, and savings are combined while streamlining financial management. It demands a great deal of communication and trust.

4. Hybrid Approach: This strategy blends aspects of separate and joint accounts. While keeping separate accounts for their own spending, couples may use joint accounts for significant purchases and savings objectives. This strategy strikes a compromise between personal freedom and group financial management.

- **Assembling a Collective Budget**

1. Evaluating Revenue and Outlays: Assess each partner's income, spending, and debts first. This evaluation offers a thorough understanding of your overall financial condition and supports the development of a sensible budget.

2. Determining Common Financial Objectives: Decide on common financial objectives, including building an emergency fund, saving for a vacation, or buying a house. Setting goals in alignment guarantees that both parties are pursuing similar objectives.

3. Assigning Cash: Decide how much of each partner's salary will go towards savings, personal spending, and joint expenses. To guarantee that financial contributions are just and equal, have a clear allocation plan.

4. Tracking Spending: Keep an eye on your spending and your budget by using applications or tools for budgeting. You may find areas for improvement and make sure you stay on track with your financial goals by often examining your budget.

- **Controlling Joint Costs**

1. Determining Common Expenses: Enumerate every shared expense, including utilities, groceries, rent or mortgage, and car expenses. Knowing these costs can help you decide how much to take out of your joint account.

2. Developing a Payment plan: Establish a shared expense payment plan to guarantee timely payments and frequent account reconciliation. Maintaining financial stability and avoiding late penalties are made easier with a regular schedule.

3. Managing Unusual Expenses: Make a budget for sporadic expenses like yearly maintenance or insurance charges. To prevent financial burden when these expenses come, save aside money in advance to cover them.

4. Resolving Inconsistencies: Address conflicts or inconsistencies over shared spending in an amicable and constructive manner. Maintaining financial harmony and addressing challenges are made easier with regular communication.

- **Management of Debt**

1. Evaluating Total Debt: Examine the indebtedness of both partners, taking into account mortgages, credit card balances, personal loans, and school loans. Having a clear understanding of total debt levels aids in creating a repayment plan.

2. Debt Repayment Plan Creation: Create a strategy for handling and paying down combined debt. Sort your loans by interest rate and make a payback plan that works with your spending plan.

3. Discourse Regarding Debt: Talk openly and honestly about debt, recognising the roles and responsibilities of each partner in repaying the debt. Having open lines of communication makes handling money problems and averting disputes easier.

4. Obtaining Expert Guidance: If debt management becomes too much to handle, think about consulting a credit counsellor or financial advisor. Effective debt management and financial planning solutions can be obtained with professional assistance.

- **Retaining Personal Financial Independence**

1. Respecting Personal Financial Objectives: It's critical to respect each partner's unique financial objectives and desires when combining finances. Make sure that within the agreed-upon financial framework, personal ambitions are taken into account and encouraged.

2. Maintaining Separate Accounts: If employing a hybrid strategy, keep separate accounts for your interests in money and personal expenses. This approach lets people manage pooled finances independently.

3. Encouraging Financial Independence: Persuade each partner to keep their financial independence by carrying on with account management, individual retirement plan investments, and goal-setting.

4. Continuous Financial Monitoring: Plan frequent financial check-ins to look over your joint accounts, evaluate how well you're doing towards your objectives, and deal with any issues. Having regular conversations aids in identifying possible problems and preserving financial alignment.

- **Resolving Conflicts Regarding Finances**

1. Open Communication: Encourage frank and transparent dialogue around financial issues. Any disputes or issues should be resolved quickly and amicably, with an emphasis on discovering answers as opposed to assigning blame.

2. Looking for Settlement: If problems with money don't go away, think about getting counselling or mediation. Discussions can be facilitated and objective views can be provided by an impartial third party.

3. Making concessions and adjusting: Be prepared to make concessions and modify your financial plans if necessary. Achieving common financial objectives and preserving harmony are facilitated by adaptability and readiness to modify plans.

4. Establishing Transparency and Trust: Establishing openness and trust is crucial to the success of financial integration. Make sure that both partners participate in decision-making and have access to financial information.

One of the most important steps towards creating a united financial destiny as a partnership is combining funds. Couples can lay the groundwork for financial independence by evaluating each other's financial history, making a joint budget, allocating costs, and managing debt. The financial partnership is further strengthened by encouraging open communication, resolving problems, and preserving individual financial autonomy. Couples can work together to accomplish their financial goals and create a secure financial future by carefully planning ahead and cooperating.

➢ Combining vs. Separating Finances: Benefits and Drawbacks

Couples who desire to combine their finances must determine whether to keep separate financial systems or combine all of their assets and accounts. Each strategy has pros and cons of its own, and the best option will rely on the couple's financial objectives, interpersonal dynamics, and personal preferences. Couples can make the greatest financial and relational decisions by being aware of the benefits and drawbacks of combining or dividing their finances.

- **Combining Funds**

☐ **Positives:**

1. Streamlined Financial Management: Merging accounts simplifies money management. Couples may effortlessly monitor and oversee their income, expenses, and savings all in one location with joint accounts. This makes financial planning, bill payment, and budgeting easier.

2. Combined Financial Objectives: Financial goal-setting is frequently approached more unifiedly when finances are merged. Together, a couple might work towards common goals like emergency fund building, retirement planning, or house savings. Financial strategies and priorities are brought into alignment with this cooperative approach.

3. Improved Openness: Transparency between couples is fostered via joint accounts and combined funds. Since all parties have access to the same financial data, there is less chance of miscommunication or financial secrecy, which helps foster confidence.

4. Simpler Ways to Make Financial Decisions: Having your finances together makes financial decision-making easier. Together, a couple may decide how much to spend, save, and invest, which can ease financial planning and minimise arguments.

5. Potential Tax Advantages: Combining funds may result in tax advantages such filing jointly, which may result in credits or deductions. Furthermore, the couple may be eligible for specific financial advantages or assistance programs based on their combined income.

☐ **Drawbacks:**

1. Decline in Financial Autonomy: One's financial liberty may be lost when finances are combined. Less control over each partner's personal savings and expenditures can cause disagreements or discontent.

2. The Possibility of Conflicts: Combining accounts can highlight disparities in spending patterns, debt repayment techniques, and financial behaviours. If these differences are not discussed honestly and constructively, they may cause arguments or stress.

3. Debt-related complications: Combining finances might be difficult if one partner has a lot of debt. Debt entanglements on joint accounts could affect the credit scores and financial health of both parties.

4. Intricacies Associated with Different Financial Interests: Coordination and further planning may be needed when combining funds if one person has distinct financial interests or investments. It might be difficult to strike a balance between shared financial goals and personal interests.

5. Risks to the Law and Finances: Combining funds can put both couples at danger financially and legally, particularly if they split up or get divorced. The split of property and cash may be made more difficult by joint accounts and shared assets.

- **Dividing Up the Finances**

☐ **Positives:**

1. Maintained self-reliance in finances: Each spouse can continue to be in charge of their own finances by keeping their funds separate. This method encourages different spending inclinations, savings plans, and financial objectives.

2. Decreased Tension Regarding Expenditure: Conflicts over individual spending and financial decisions can be reduced when funds are kept apart. Because each partner is in charge of their own finances, there are less chances for arguments on how to handle money.

3. Streamlined Debt Administration: Each partner is accountable for their own debts if they have separate accounts. This can make debt management easier and stop one partner's debt from negatively affecting the other's financial status.

4. Transparent Allocation of Resources and Debts: A clean split of assets and obligations is made possible by separate finances. Each partner's assets and financial obligations are clearly defined in the event of a split or divorce, which could make the legal procedure easier.

5. Personalised Financial Plans: Having independent financial accounts enables each spouse to create and adhere to their own financial plans. This might be especially helpful if partners have varied risk tolerances, investment philosophies, or financial objectives.

☐ **Drawbacks:**

1. Intricate Financial Administration: Separate financial management might be more difficult, especially when it comes to common costs like groceries, rent, and utilities. It can take time for couples to arrange and keep track of these expenses individually.

2. The Possibility of Inequal Contributions: Disagreements regarding contributions to joint expenses can arise from having separate finances. One spouse may believe that they are giving more or less than the other if there isn't a clear method in place for allocating finances.

3. Restricted Financial Cooperation: The financial synergy that results from combining resources may be reduced by keeping finances apart. Couples who combine their financial holdings may lose out on possibilities to optimise investments, savings, or tax advantages.

4. Difficulties with Shared Objectives: It can be more difficult to accomplish shared financial objectives, like retirement planning or preparing for a large purchase, when funds are separate. In order to achieve their shared goals, couples must coordinate their efforts and make sure that both partners are on board.

5. Insufficient Openness: Reduced financial transparency between partners could be the outcome of separate finances. If financial information is not disclosed honestly, this could result in miscommunications or a lack of trust.

- **Achieving the Appropriate Balance**

The choice to combine or keep separate funds ultimately comes down to the particular needs and preferences of the couple. Many couples choose a hybrid strategy, incorporating aspects of the two approaches to strike a balance between individual autonomy and shared financial management. For instance, a couple may use a joint account for common costs and savings objectives, but maintain separate accounts for personal spending.

When deciding whether to combine or separate funds, open communication, mutual respect, and a clear grasp of each partner's financial habits and aspirations are crucial. To make sure that their strategy supports both their financial well-being and the harmony of their relationship, couples should assess their financial arrangements on a regular basis and make adjustments as appropriate.

Couples can improve their financial partnership, achieve their financial goals, and create a stable financial future for themselves by carefully weighing the benefits and drawbacks of combining their finances or keeping them separate.

➤ Making a Combined Budget

One of the most important things a couple can do to move towards financial stability and independence is to create a common budget. A well-organised joint budget promotes openness and collaboration in financial planning in addition to aiding in the management of shared spending. This is a thorough tutorial on how to draft a successful joint budget:

1. Honest Communication

Setting Financial Objectives:

- Talk About Financial Priorities: Start by discussing your financial objectives in an open and honest manner. This covers both short-term and long-term objectives, such as retirement planning and vacation savings. Make certain that both spouses are aware of one other's financial goals.

- Identify Common Objectives: Decide which financial objectives—like purchasing a house, paying for school, or setting up an emergency fund—are shared. Having these objectives in line will make it easier to develop a budget that meets the needs and ambitions of both partners.

Comprehending Financial Circumstances:

- Exchanging Financial Data: Disclosure of the partners' present financial circumstances, including income, expenses, obligations, and assets, is required. Complete transparency facilitates the creation of a precise and practical budget.

- Talk About Spending Patterns: Discuss personal spending preferences and habits. Setting reasonable budget categories and restrictions can be aided by having a thorough understanding of each partner's spending habits.

2. Determine Your Earnings

Combine Income Sources:

- Calculate Total Income: Total up all of your revenue sources, including investments, freelancing, salary, and any other sources. This gives a clear image of the entire revenue of the home that can be used for budgeting.

- Take Variability into Account: If one or both partners earns money from commissions or freelance work, calculate an average monthly revenue to use in your budget.

Find Net Income:

- Deduct Taxes and Other Outlays: Make sure the budget accurately represents the amount available for spending and saving by using the net income figure, which is the amount left over after taxes and deductions.

3. Sort and Sort through Expenses

List Monthly Shared Expenses:

- List Monthly Fixed Expenses: Add monthly fixed costs (rent, mortgage, utilities, insurance, and loan payments, for example) to the list.

- Variable Expenses: Take into consideration variable costs like groceries, eating out, entertainment, and personal hygiene.

Individual Spending:

- Separate Personal Expenses: When it comes to things like clothing, hobbies, or personal gifts, each partner should keep track of their own spending accounts. This aids in controlling shared spending while preserving financial independence.

Assess and Distribute:

- Cost Groups: Make categories and allot a certain amount to every kind of spending. Make sure that fixed and variable costs are included in the budget.

4. Establish a Shared Account

Select a Joint Account:

- Choosing the Correct Account: Create a joint checking account with the express purpose of handling shared spending. Income should be deposited into this account, and both partners should utilise it to pay bills and other expenses.

- Determine The Contribution Amounts: Taking into account each partner's income and financial obligations, decide how much each will contribute to the joint account. Depending on what suits both spouses most, this could be a fixed sum of money or a percentage of earnings.

It is important to manage contributions made to the joint account by making sure that both partners make monthly deposits of the agreed-upon amounts. If at all possible, set up automatic transfers to streamline the procedure.

- Record Account Utilisation: Examine the joint account on a regular basis to monitor expenditure and make sure that costs are being handled in line with the budget.

5. Monitor Expenditure and Modifications

Keep an Eye on Budget Adherence:

- **Track Expenses:** Keep tabs on expenditures relative to the budget using apps or budgeting tools. Frequent observation enables prompt corrections and assists in identifying any discrepancies.

- **Examine and Modify:** Make sure the budget reflects any changes in income or expenses by reviewing it on a regular basis. As necessary, change the categories and amounts to keep inside your budget.

Repeatedly Communicate:

- **Check-ins with the Budget:** Call frequent meetings to go over the budget and talk about any changes or problems with the finances. Concerns can be addressed and both parties can stay in agreement when there is open communication.

- **Appreciate Achievements:** Celebrate and recognise your financial accomplishments and milestones.

Acknowledging successes helps strengthen constructive financial habits and increase motivation.

6. Handling Inconsistencies in Finance

Handling Disagreements:

- **Open Dialogue:** Discuss differences of opinion over the budget of expenditures in an amicable and courteous manner. Make an effort to come up with ideas that benefit all parties.

- **Seek Equilibrium:** If necessary, be prepared to make concessions and changes to the budget. It takes teamwork and flexibility to keep a collaborative budgeting process going strong.

Expert Consultants:

- **Money Guidance:** If disputes don't go away or the budget is complicated, you might want to consult a financial expert. Seeking professional advice can yield insightful information and assist in resolving financial concerns.

7. Preserving Your Financial Well-Being

Emergency Fund:

- **Build Savings:** Make sure that contributions to an emergency fund are included in the budget. This fund offers a safety net in case of unforeseen costs or crises.

- **Consistent Contributions:** To guarantee steady savings, set up automatic transfers to the emergency fund.

Planning for Retirement:

- **Investments for Retirement:** Set aside money for retirement savings through IRA or 401(k) account contributions, for example. Contribute on a regular basis to retirement accounts as a way to secure your financial future.

Long-Term Objectives:

- **Future Planning:** Include long-term financial objectives in the budget, such as home, school, or vacation savings. Review and modify your savings targets on a regular basis.

One of the first steps for a couple looking to become financially independent and accumulate wealth together is making a shared budget. Couples can establish a budget that supports their shared financial objectives by being upfront with each other, evaluating income, classifying expenses, opening a joint account, monitoring spending, and resolving differences. A strong financial partnership and a stable financial future can result from routine budget review and adjustment, as well as a dedication to honest communication and compromise.

➢ Financial Roles and Responsibilities

Achieving financial objectives and preserving harmony in a partnership depend heavily on clearly defining and comprehending financial duties and responsibilities. Couples may make sure their financial planning is efficient, fair, and in line with their goals by outlining exactly who is in charge of what when it comes to money management. A thorough approach to assigning financial roles and responsibilities in a relationship may be found here:

1. Determining Financial Positions

Knowing Each Partner's Strengths:

- Evaluating Skills and Knowledge: Find out what areas each partner excels at managing their debt, investing, and budgeting. Use these abilities to allocate roles that correspond with the areas of expertise and interests of each individual.

- **Determine Your Preferences:** Think about the preferences and comfort levels of each partner when it comes to certain financial chores. For example, one spouse might be more interested in managing investments than the other in handling day-to-day spending.

Specific Roles Defining:

- **Main Financial Manager:** As the principal financial manager, one partner may be in charge of managing investments, keeping tabs on spending, and creating budgets. Strong organisational abilities and familiarity with finances are needed for this function.

- **Adjunct Financial Assistance:** The other partner might take on a supportive role, helping with things like checking financial statements, offering advice on financial choices, and making sure the budget is followed.

2. Determining Accountabilities

Manage the Budget:

- Create and Update the Budget: Assign someone to be in charge of updating and generating the family budget. This entails keeping tabs on earnings, classifying spending, and adjusting as necessary.

- Keeping an Eye on Spending: Assign someone to keep an eye on daily expenditures to make sure they stay within the budget. Review financial transactions on a regular basis and resolve any disparities.

Payment of Bills and Debt Management:

- Bill Handling: Assign who will be in charge of paying rent or a mortgage, utilities, and insurance on time. Automated payment setup can make this process easier.

- Managing Debt: Assign duty for managing debt, which includes monitoring interest rates, making loan payments, and creating plans for debt reduction.

Investments and Savings:

- **Contributions to Savings:** Decide who will be in charge of managing contributions to savings accounts for short-term savings objectives, retirement accounts, and emergency reserves.

- **Venture Selections:** Assign duty for managing investments, which includes looking into prospects, keeping an eye on results, and choosing assets. Make sure the investing strategy is communicated to both partners.

3. Responsibility and Decision-Making

Collaborative Decision-Making:

- **Key Financial Decisions:** Create a procedure for deciding on important financial decisions, including buying a house or making significant investments. Make sure that both partners participate in and approve of the decisions made in these matters.

- **Consistent Conversations:** Call frequent financial meetings to go over the goals and budget and make any required adjustments. Transparency is promoted and agreement amongst the partners is guaranteed by open communication.

Accountability and Transparency:

- **Tracking Progress:** Keep tabs on the status of financial objectives and make sure that obligations are fulfilled. Examine budget performance and financial statements on a regular basis.

- **Resolving Concerns:** In the event that financial problems or disparities occur, resolve them quickly and cooperatively. Concentrate on resolving issues and modifying roles and duties as needed.

4. Juggling Different Tasks

Fair Allocation:

- **Equitable Distribution:** - Make sure that financial obligations are allocated equitably taking into account the abilities, schedules, and preferences of each partner. Try to divide the work equally so that no spouse feels overworked or underappreciated.

- **Adaptability:** Have the ability to modify duties as necessary. It could be necessary to reassign tasks and responsibilities due to life changes like a new job or a change in financial objectives.

Support and Cooperation:

- **Mutual Support:** Encourage and support one another in handling financial obligations. Acknowledge the work of each partner and share in triumphs as a team.

- **Collaborative Approach:** Address financial obstacles and accomplish goals as a team. Financial management is strengthened and a sense of collaboration is fostered through collaborative decision-making.

5. Growth and Education in Finance

Continuous Learning:

- Financial Literacy: Motivate both partners to partake in continuous financial literacy. To increase your financial literacy and abilities, study books on finance, enrol in classes, or attend workshops.

- Remaining Up to Date: Keep up with changes in the economy, investment possibilities, and financial laws. Keep your financial knowledge up to date so you can make wise judgements.

Skill Development:

- Personal Growth: Assist one another in acquiring financial knowledge and abilities. Provide tools or support to a partner who lacks experience in a certain area so they can get better.

- **Goal Alignment:** Constantly match changing personal and financial goals with financial duties and responsibilities. Adjust positions as necessary to reflect shifts in your goals and financial status.

6. Handling Difficulties

Handling Disagreements:

- **Open Communication:** Have courteous and open discussions when handling disputes regarding financial positions or responsibilities. Concentrate on identifying points of agreement and pursuing solutions that will satisfy both parties.

- **Conflict Resolution:** To resolve financial conflicts, put conflict resolution techniques into practice. Try to comprehend one another's viewpoints and work together to find solutions.

Seeking Professional Advice:

- **Financial experts:** Seek advice on difficult financial concerns from financial experts if necessary. Expert counsel can help settle disputes and enhance money management.

– **Advise:** If there are ongoing financial difficulties, think about financial counselling or therapy. Expert assistance can improve financial harmony and open up productive dialogues.

For couples hoping to become financially independent and accumulate wealth jointly, clearly defining duties and obligations in terms of money is crucial. Couples can manage their finances and work towards shared financial goals by defining precise tasks, focussing on each other's strengths, and encouraging open communication. Maintaining financial success and peace requires sharing resources, keeping one another up to date on finances, and balancing duties. A solid and cooperative financial partnership is ensured by navigating obstacles with flexibility and getting expert assistance when necessary.

Chapter Three

Creating Wealth Together

Building wealth as a partnership takes teamwork, common objectives, and a dedication to each other's financial development in addition to simple money management. Long-term financial success can be established by coordinating your financial strategy and working towards shared goals. A number of essential elements are involved in this process, such as creating a comprehensive financial plan, establishing shared financial objectives, and keeping lines of communication open throughout the wealth-building process. Here's a thorough approach on helping couples accumulate wealth together:

1. Determining Combined Financial Objectives

☐ **Common Vision:**

- **Determine Common Goals:** Talk about your long-term financial goals together first. These could be things like house ownership, retirement savings, paying for kids' schooling, or vacations. It is guaranteed that both partners are pursuing the same objectives when there is a common vision.

- **Establish Clear Objectives:** Convert your big ambitions into attainable, quantifiable objectives. For instance, state your objective as something like "we aim to save $500,000 for retirement by age 65" rather than just "we want to save for retirement."

☐ **Achievements, both short- and long-term:**

- **Short-Term Objectives:** These are attainable objectives, like paying off credit card debt or setting aside money for a trip, that can be completed in the next one to three years. Setting short-term objectives gives you a sense of accomplishment and helps you stay motivated.

- **Long-Term Objectives:** Long-term objectives go beyond three years and can involve major turning points such as owning a property or building a sizable retirement account. These objectives call for more preparation and consistent work.

2. Formulating an All-inclusive Budget

☐ **Co-Budgeting:**

- **Collaborative Budget Development:** Create a collaborative budget that details your combined income, costs, savings, and contributions to investments. Your mutual priorities and financial goals should be reflected in this budget.

- **Tracing Expenses:** Make sure your expenditure is in line with your budget by keeping a regular check on it. To track and arrange your spending, make use of tools like spreadsheets and budgeting applications.

☐ **Investments and Savings:**

- **Emergency Fund:** Establish and keep an emergency fund to deal with unforeseen costs. Try to accumulate three to six months' worth of living expenses in an account that is easily accessible.

- **Strategy for Investment:** Create an investment plan that is in line with your financial objectives, time horizon, and risk tolerance. Think about making real estate, mutual funds, equities, and bonds investments in a diverse portfolio.

☐ **Management of Debt:**

- **Debt Reduction Strategy:** Formulate a strategy to oversee and minimise any current debt. Set aside money for high-interest debt repayment (credit card bills, for example) and make regular loan payments.

- **Avoiding New Debt:** Put plans in place to prevent taking on new debt, like setting up a savings account for major purchases and judicious use of credit cards.

3. Cooperation and Effective Communication

☐ **Monthly Financial Meetings:**

- **Planned Conversations:** Call frequent financial meetings to discuss any issues, go over your budget, and monitor your goals' progress. These sessions offer a forum for candid discussion of financial issues and the implementation of required changes.

- **Review of Progress:** Analyse your progress towards reaching your financial objectives throughout these meetings. Celebrate your accomplishments and, if necessary, review your plan.

☐ **Dispute Resolution:**

- **Respectful and Honest Communication:** Handle any financial disputes or issues with courtesy and candour. Instead of placing blame, concentrate on coming up with solutions.

- **Flexibility and Compromise:** Be prepared to make concessions and modify your budget if needed. Being flexible keeps you both on the same page financially and in sync with your objectives.

4. Making Use of Collaborative Finance Tools

☐ **Collaborative Accounts and Investment Tools:**

- **Collaborative Bank Accounts:** Take into consideration creating cooperative bank accounts for shared spending and savings. This method guarantees openness while streamlining financial management.

- **Combined Investment Funds:** To pool money for long-term investments, use joint investment accounts. This can help you reach financial objectives more quickly and increase your capacity to invest in higher-value assets.

☐ **Money Management Tools:**

- **Budgeting Apps:** Use budgeting applications to keep tabs on your spending, oversee your spending, and assess your financial development. Shared access is enabled by many apps, making collaborative money management easier.

- **Platforms for Investment:** Make use of investing solutions that enable joint accounts or team investment management. These platforms frequently offer resources for monitoring and evaluating investments.

5. Strategies for Long-Term Wealth Creation

☐ **Planning for Retirement:**

- **Retirement Funds:** Make contributions to retirement accounts like IRAs, Roth IRAs, and 401(k)s. To optimise your retirement savings, make use of tax breaks and employer-matched contributions.

- **Assets for Retirement:** Specify your retirement objectives, such as your ideal retirement age, way of life, and required income. Modify your investing and savings plan to achieve these objectives.

☐ **Real Estate and Property:**

- **Homeownership:** Take into account buying a house as a long-term investment. Before buying a house, assess your financial situation and make sure your goals are in line with your budget.

- **Investments in Real Estate:** Examine your options for investing in real estate, including rental homes and real estate investment trusts (REITs). Your investment portfolio can be diversified and passive income can be generated from real estate.

☐ **Trusts and Wills:**

- **Estate Planning:** To guarantee that your assets are allocated in accordance with your preferences, create trusts and wills. Estate planning safeguards your money and takes care of your loved ones.

- **Designations of Beneficiaries:** Examine and amend beneficiary names on investment accounts, insurance policies, and retirement plans, among other accounts.

6. Preserving Flexibility and Financial Health

☐ **Annual Reviews:**

- **Regular Financial Reviews:** Review your financial plan once a year to evaluate your accomplishments, modify your objectives, and make any required adjustments. Frequent reviews guarantee that your plan stays in line with your changing objectives and demands.

- **Switching with the Times:** Be ready to modify your financial plan in the event that something in your life happens, such as a job loss, an increase in income, or significant expenses. Sustaining financial stability requires flexibility.

☐ **Ongoing Education:**

- **Money Management:** Spend some time studying investing, wealth-building, and personal finance. To make wise decisions, keep up with industry developments and best practices in finance.

- **Expert Counsel:** Consult professionals or financial consultants for guidance as necessary. You can improve your efforts to accumulate wealth and manage challenging financial circumstances with the assistance of a professional.

Establishing goals, making decisions, and managing finances collaboratively are all essential to building wealth as a partnership. Couples can work towards shared financial success by setting clear financial goals, making an extensive financial plan, and keeping lines of communication open. Achieving and maintaining financial independence requires utilising shared financial instruments, putting long-term wealth-building tactics into practice, and routinely assessing your financial strategy. Couples can enjoy the fruits of their joint labours and establish a solid financial foundation by being dedicated, cooperative, and lifelong learners.

➢ Investment Techniques for Duos

Coordination, communication, and a shared strategy are necessary when investing as a pair, but it also presents special potential for wealth accumulation and reaching financial objectives. This is a thorough guide on investment strategies that can assist couples in coordinating their financial objectives and coming to well-informed investment decisions:

1. Setting Up Investment Objectives

☐ **Common Goals:**

- **Common Objectives:** Talk about your common investment goals first. These could be setting up a retirement account, saving for a down payment on a home, or setting up a fund for a child's education. It is easier to make sure that your investing strategy meets the aims of both partners when you are aware of each other's objectives.

- Determined Time Ranges: Various objectives will have varying time frames. A down payment on a home, for example, might be a short- to medium-term objective, whereas retirement funds are for a longer period of time. Adjust your investment strategy according to these timelines.

☐ **Tolerance for Risk:**

- Evaluate Your Joint Risk Tolerance: Ascertain the amount of risk you are both willing to accept on your assets by calculating your joint risk tolerance. A number of variables, including age, income, financial objectives, and degree of comfort with market volatility, should be taken into account.

- **Equipped Method:** Strike a balance between stable, low-risk investments and high-risk ones, which might yield larger rewards. While pursuing growth, a diversified portfolio aids in risk management.

2. Formulating a Collective Investment Plan

☐ **Asset Allocation:**

- **Diversification:** Invest in a variety of asset classes, including cash, bonds, stocks, and real estate. This strategy can increase overall returns while spreading risk. The effects of a single investment's poor performance are lessened by a well-diversified portfolio.

- **Diversification by Geography:** To take advantage of chances for global expansion and lessen the effects of local economic downturns, think about investing in both domestic and foreign markets.

☐ **Venture Vehicles:**

- **Retirement Accounts:** Fund retirement plans such as IRAs, Roth IRAs, or 401(k)s. To optimise retirement savings, make use of tax breaks and employer-matched contributions. SEP IRAs and Solo 401(k)s are two possibilities to think about if one or both partners work for themselves.

- **Accounts Payable:** For objectives outside of retirement accounts, use taxable investment accounts. Although these accounts are subject to capital gains taxes, they provide greater freedom with regard to withdrawals and investing options.

- **Accounts for Education Savings:** Consider accounts like 529 plans or Coverdell Education Savings Accounts (ESAs), which provide tax benefits for educational expenses, if you're planning for your children's future education.

3. Joint Venture Administration

☐ **Collaborative Investment Accounts:**

- **Account Opening:** Take into consideration creating cooperative investment accounts to combine funds for common financial objectives. Joint accounts streamline the process of managing your finances and offer transparency.

- **Venture Selections:** Make joint investing decisions, making sure that each partner participates in selecting investments and keeping track of results. By working together, you can better match your assets to your risk tolerance and common objectives.

☐ **Regular Evaluations:**

- **Timed Evaluations:** Review your investment portfolio on a regular basis to evaluate performance, adapt for market conditions, and rebalance as necessary. Decide on a timetable for these reviews, such as yearly or quarterly.

- **Switching with the Times:** If your income, work status, or other significant life events change, be ready to modify your investment approach. Your investing strategy will stay in line with your changing needs if it is flexible.

4. Risk Management for Investments

☐ **Security Net Construction:**

- Emergency Fund: Keep an emergency reserve on hand to pay for unforeseen costs. This fund ought to be conveniently accessible and kept apart from your investing accounts. Having an emergency fund helps you stay stable financially and lessens the need to take advantage of market dips.

☐ **Coverage:**

- Investment Protection: Make sure you have enough insurance, including disability, life, and health insurance. In the event of unanticipated circumstances that can jeopardise your financial security, insurance safeguards your investments and your financial health.

☐ **Volatility of the Market:**

- Long-Term View: When making investments, have a strong emphasis on the long term. It is typical for markets to fluctuate, but your long-term investing approach shouldn't be derailed by momentary volatility. Adhere to your strategy and refrain from acting rashly in response to transient market fluctuations.

5. Investment Plans for Particular Objectives

☐ **Home Savings:**

- Down Payment Reserve: When saving for a house, think about investing in low- to medium-risk securities that strike a balance between capital preservation and growth. Stability and liquidity can be obtained through high-yield savings accounts or short-term bond funds.

- Investment in Home Equity: After you buy a house, think about making investments in upgrades or other real estate to further your attempts to accumulate wealth.

☐ **Retirement Savings Development:**

- **Long-Term Growth:** For retirement savings, concentrate on long-term growth options like stocks, mutual funds, and exchange-traded funds (ETFs). Over time, these investments usually yield larger returns, which can contribute to the accumulation of a sizable retirement fund.

- **Integration:** To reduce risk and increase returns, diversify the assets in your retirement portfolio over a range of asset classes. When you grow closer to retirement age, take into account target-date funds that automatically modify their asset allocation.

☐ **Education Savings Plans:**

- **Funding Education:** To save money for school costs, use education savings accounts (ESAs), such as Coverdell ESAs or 529 plans. These accounts can be invested in a diverse portfolio to increase over time and offer tax advantages.

- **Grants and Scholarships:** Investigate grant and scholarship options to augment your funds and lessen the cost of your education.

6. Seeking Expert Guidance

☐ **Financial Advisors:**

- **Consulting Experts:** To assist you in creating and carrying out your investment strategy, think about speaking with a financial advisor or other investment specialist. Advisors are able to offer tailored advice according to your risk tolerance and financial objectives.

- **Charging Schedules:** Recognise the financial advisors' fee structures and compensation schemes. Select an advisor who provides transparent pricing and shares your interests.

☐ **Learning and Research:**

- **Ongoing Education:** Remain up to date on financial strategy, market trends, and investing possibilities. You can improve your understanding of investments and make wise judgements by reading books, going to seminars, or enrolling in online courses.

Investing together provides a means of achieving common financial objectives and building wealth. Couples can improve their financial development and stability by aligning their investment goals, creating a thorough plan, and managing risks well. The secret to successful investment management is constant education, collaborative decision-making, and regular communication. Couples can successfully manage the challenges of investing and create a prosperous financial future if they have a well-organised investment plan and a dedication to collaboration.

➢ Budgeting and Savings Together

Particularly for couples with shared financial duties and objectives, saving and budgeting are essential to reaching financial independence and accumulating wealth. Cooperation in financial management can result in better budgeting, more disciplined saving, and eventually, a more secure financial future. This is a thorough guide on how to budget and save money as a couple:

1. Establishing Joint Financial Objectives

☐ **Identifying Common Objectives:**

- **Short- and Long-Term Objectives:** First, talk about and decide on your short- and long-term financial objectives. Long-term objectives can include saving for retirement or purchasing a home, while short-term objectives might be saving for a trip or a new automobile.

- **Setting Priorities:** Set your goals in order of significance and urgency. Decide which objectives to prioritise first and how much money and effort will be needed for each.

☐ **Building a Vision:**

- **Depicting Achievement:** Develop a common understanding of your financial future. Both partners benefit from this visualisation in terms of maintaining motivation and goal alignment. To help you achieve your goals, use visual aids such as vision boards, graphs, and charts.

2. Creating a Collaborative Budget

☐ **Combining Income and Expenses:**

- **Tracking Income:** Add up your earnings to get the total amount of money your household makes. This stage aids in precisely evaluating your financial status and creating a budget.

- **Advertising Charges:** Keep track of every household spending, including variable costs like groceries and entertainment as well as fixed costs like rent, mortgage, and utilities. Make sure you are comprehensive so that no cost is missed.

☐ **Building a Budget Plan:**

- **Assigning Funds:**** Distribute money according to your total income to each area of spending. Make sure your budget accounts for savings and discretionary expenditures, as well as your priorities and aspirations.

- **Using Tools for Budgeting:** Track your spending and keep an eye on your budget by using apps and tools for budgeting. You can stay organised with the use of programs like Mint, YNAB (You Need A Budget), or even basic spreadsheets.

3. Making a Plan for Savings

☐ **Setting Savings Objectives:**

- **Emergency Fund:** Give careful consideration to accumulating an emergency fund that can cover living expenditures for at least three to six months. In the event of unforeseen circumstances such as job loss or medical difficulties, this fund offers financial protection.

- **Savings Aim-Specific:** Set aside money in savings for particular objectives, such a vacation or a down payment on a home. To keep your money organised and monitor your progress, create distinct savings accounts for each of these objectives.

☐ **Automated Transfers:**

- **Automating Savings:** To guarantee regular contributions to your savings accounts, set up automated payments. By automating saves, one can foster a savings habit and lessen their urge to spend money that could be saved.

- **Modifying Donations:** Review and modify your savings contributions on a regular basis in light of shifting goals, costs, or income. When you can, such as after a bonus or raise, increase your savings contributions.

4. Handling Collaborative Accounts and Costs

☐ **Joint Accounts:**

- **Shared Bank Accounts:** Take into consideration establishing a joint savings or checking account for common spending and objectives. This method guarantees financial transparency and streamlines financial administration.

- **Maintaining Individual Accounts:** Maintain separate accounts for your own expenses and financial autonomy. Individual accounts provide you independence while keeping a single account for shared duties.

☐ **Expense Tracking:**

- **Tracking Shared spending:** Keep tabs on shared spending using spreadsheets or applications to make sure each partner contributes equitably. This openness guarantees that both parties are in agreement and helps avoid misunderstandings.

- **Compromise:** To guarantee accuracy and resolve any differences, reconcile your accounts on a regular basis. This phase keeps your finances in balance and makes sure your budget is on track.

5. Improving Exchange of Financial Information

☐ **Scheduled Meetings:**

- **Regular Discussions:** Set up frequent financial meetings to go over your savings, investments, and budget. These sessions offer a chance to go over financial objectives, deal with any problems, and make any necessary corrections.

- **Initiate Discussion:** Encourage honest dialogue regarding money-related issues. Being open and honest about your financial status promotes mutual understanding and prevents misunderstandings.

☐ **Compromise and Negotiation:**

- **Resolving Disagreements:** When making financial decisions, be ready to bargain and make concessions. Recognise that the two spouses could have distinct spending patterns and priorities when it comes to money, and collaborate to develop solutions that satisfy both of you.

- **Looking for Expert Assistance:** Seek advice from a counsellor or financial expert if disputes don't go away. Experts can offer unbiased counsel and assistance in identifying solutions that support the objectives of both parties.

6. Examining and Modifying Financial Plans

☐ **Regular Evaluations:**

- **Money Check-Ins:** Regularly assess your savings account, investment portfolio, and budget. Frequent check-ins assist in evaluating your financial development and implementing any required changes.

- **Switching with the Times:** Be adaptable and modify your financial strategy to account for variations in your income, expenses, or personal situation. As necessary, adjust your savings targets and budget to take into account your present circumstances.

☐ **Celebrating Success:**

- **Acknowledgement of Achievement** Commemorate successes and financial benchmarks collectively. Acknowledging and recognising your accomplishments keeps you motivated and reinforces wise financial decisions.

- **Modifying Objectives:** Set new objectives as you meet them and modify your financial plans accordingly. Setting and establishing goals on a regular basis helps to keep you motivated and focused on your financial path.

7. Utilising Technology to Manage Finances

☐ **Budgeting applications:**

- **Using Technology:** To make tracking, budgeting, and saving easier, use applications for financial management and budgeting. Financial management can be made easier with the help of apps like Mint, YNAB, or Personal Capital, which also reveal information about your saving and spending habits.

☐ **Money Tracking Tools:**

- **Expense Tracking:** Sort and keep an eye on your expenses with the help of expense tracking tools. This assists in pinpointing areas where you can reduce expenses and devote more resources to investments and savings.

- Asset Monitoring: To keep track of your progress towards your financial objectives, set up goal-tracking features. Technology can help you stay motivated by giving you visual representations of your work.

Building wealth and reaching financial freedom need teamwork in saving and budgeting. Couples can effectively manage their finances and work towards a secure financial future by setting shared financial objectives, creating a joint budget, creating a savings strategy, and keeping lines of communication open.

Maintaining financial harmony and attaining long-term success can be facilitated by conducting regular evaluations, utilising technology, and resolving conflicts together. Couples can improve their financial well-being and create a wealthy future by working together and implementing a sound financial strategy.

➢ Setting Up Major Financial Objectives

Setting and completing key financial goals is essential to become financially independent and accumulate wealth as a partnership. Large-scale financial objectives like home ownership, college funding, and a comfortable retirement need for meticulous preparation, self-control, and cooperation. Here is a thorough guide to assist couples in setting and achieving their main financial objectives:

1. Determining Important Financial Objectives

☐ **Setting Objectives:**

- **Details:** Begin by outlining your main financial objectives. To avoid generic goals such as "save for a house," one could establish a specific objective like "save $50,000 for a down payment on a house within five years."

- **Time Horizon:** Establish the duration of each objective. Long-term (5–30 years) goals might include retirement or home ownership, whereas short-term (1-3 years) goals might be vacations or minor house upgrades.

☐ **Aligning Goals:**

- **Shared Vision:** Make sure that the financial objectives are shared and accepted by both partners. Having your goals in alignment promotes cohesion and facilitates efficient goal-achieving.

- **Order of importance:** Sort your goals according to urgency and priority. Determine the priorities for addressing each goal and the best way to distribute resources.

2. Formulating an Extensive Budget

☐ **Budget Allocation:**

- **Setting Aside Funds:** Set aside a certain amount of money from your budget for every significant financial objective. For instance, if you want to save $50,000 for a down payment, figure out how much you'll need to save every month to get there in the allotted time.

- **Changes to the Budget:** To meet your savings objectives, modify your spending plan. This could entail reallocating money from other areas or cutting back on discretionary spending.

☐ **Savings Accounts:**

- **Accounts Dedicated:** Create distinct savings accounts for every important objective. This method makes it simpler to monitor your progress and keeps your money organised. Establish separate accounts, for instance, one for retirement and one for the down payment on a house.

- **Transfers Automatically:** To guarantee recurring contributions, set up automatic transfers to these savings accounts. The incentive to spend money that should be saved is lessened when savings are automated.

3. Formulating a Savings Plan

☐ **Emergency Fund:**

- **Building a Safety Net:** Make sure you have a sizable emergency fund before you start saving aggressively for big ambitions. A three to six month emergency reserve that covers living expenses avoids setbacks and offers financial security.

- **Scheduling Objectives:** As you work towards your main financial objectives, set aside money to create or maintain your emergency fund. Maintaining a balance between long-term goals and immediate security is essential.

☐ **Investment Approaches:**

- **Selecting Assets:** Select the right investment vehicles based on your time horizon. Low-risk investments such as short-term bonds or savings accounts are good choices for short-term objectives. Look at retirement accounts, mutual funds, and equities for long-term objectives.

- **Tolerance for Risk:** Determine how much risk you can afford to take, then make investments accordingly. Investments with higher risk may have higher returns, but they also have higher volatility. Match your financial objectives and degree of comfort with your investment approach.

4. Tracking and Modifying Development

☐ **Monthly Evaluations:**

- **Monitoring Advancement:** Review your progress towards each financial objective on a regular basis. To keep an eye on your investments, savings, and overall financial health, use budgeting and financial tracking tools.

- Correcting Mistakes: If your income, expenses, or goals change, be ready to modify your plan. Events in life such as a change of employment, a large purchase, or unforeseen costs may require alterations to your savings plan.

☐ **Acknowledgements:**

- Celebrating Milestones: Acknowledge accomplishments and move closer to your objectives. Acknowledging your successes increases drive and supports responsible financial practices.

- Reviewing Objectives: Make revisions to your financial plan as you discover new priorities or reach your goals. Your financial plan will always be in line with your changing demands if you set new goals or modify old ones.

5. Handling Credit and Debt

☐ **Managing Debt:**

- **Granting Debt Repayment Priority:** Paying off large debts should take precedence over making aggressive savings for important objectives. To ease financial hardship, high-interest debt—like credit card debt—should be paid off first.

- **Strategies for Debt Reduction:** Use debt repayment techniques such as the avalanche or snowball methods. Paying off debt increases one's capacity for savings and enhances financial stability.

☐ **Staying in Good Credit:**

- **Keeping an Eye on Credit Scores:** Make sure your credit report and score are accurate and note any areas that need work by checking them on a regular basis. Financial opportunities and favourable loan terms are contingent upon having a high credit score.

- **Credit Building:** Continue to practise good credit hygiene by keeping credit card balances low and paying bills on time. When requesting a mortgage, auto loan, or other financial product, having good credit is advantageous.

6. Working Together and Exchange Information

☐ **Common Responsibilities:**

- **Task Distribution:** Assign tasks and finances according to each partner's preferences and areas of strength. For instance, one partner may be in charge of budgeting and the other of investing.

- **Collaborative Effort:** Make decisions and carry out your financial plan as a team. Working together guarantees that both partners are committed to reaching your financial objectives.

☐ **Transparent Communication:**

- **Consistent Conversations:** Plan frequent conversations regarding your financial advancements, difficulties, and modifications. Maintaining financial harmony, addressing concerns, and making educated decisions are all facilitated by open communication.

- **Settling Disputes:** Find a middle ground and constructively resolve financial disputes. Compromise and an understanding of each partner's viewpoint are essential for handling disagreements and accomplishing common objectives.

7. Seeking Expert Advice

☐ **Money Advisors:**

- **Expert Consultants:** For professional advice on intricate financial concerns, think about speaking with a financial advisor. Advisors can aid with investing strategy, offer tailored guidance, and facilitate the achievement of significant financial objectives.

- **Assessing Choices:** Consider a financial advisor's credentials, costs, and services before selecting one.

Make sure their knowledge meets your needs and financial objectives.

☐ **Tax and Legal Considerations:**

- Legal Advice: Consult a lawyer for wills, estate planning, and other legal issues pertaining to your financial objectives. Making appropriate legal plans guarantees that the management of your assets follows your wishes.

- Tax Planning: Speak with a tax expert to maximise your tax plan and comprehend the effects of your financial choices. Tax planning maximises savings and reduces taxable income.

Strategic planning, good teamwork, and thorough thought are necessary when planning for significant financial objectives. Couples can work towards reaching their financial goals by setting goals, developing a thorough financial plan, deciding on a savings plan, and routinely assessing their progress. Reducing debt, working well with others, and getting expert advice all increase the chances of success. Couples can attain financial independence and create a stable financial future by implementing a methodical strategy and demonstrating a dedication to collaboration.

Chapter Four

Debt Management: Techniques for Sound Finances

One of the most important steps in becoming financially independent and preserving general financial health is managing your debt. Effective debt management for couples involves teamwork, open communication, and careful planning. This is a thorough guide to debt management that includes tactics and advice to help you overcome this significant financial obstacle.

1. Getting to Know Your Debt

Debt Assessment:
- **List of Debts:** Make a list of everything you owe, including credit cards, personal loans, mortgages, school loans, and any other bills. Make a note of each debt's outstanding amount, interest rate, minimum monthly payment, and due date.

- **Group Your Loans:** Sort your debts into low- and high-interest categories, such as credit cards and student loans or mortgages. Setting repayment priorities is aided by having a clear understanding of the type of debt you have.

Debt-to-Income Ratio:

- **Evaluating Your Debt Load:** By dividing your total monthly debt payments by your gross monthly income, you can find your debt-to-income (DTI) ratio. Your finances may be strained if your debt repayment represents a larger percentage of your income, as indicated by a high debt-to-income ratio.

- **Report on Credit:** Examine your credit report to make sure it is accurate and to find any inconsistencies. An extensive synopsis of your credit history and ongoing debts can be found in your credit report.

2. Giving Debt Repayment Priority

- **Snowball Method:** Prioritise paying off your lowest debt first and make the minimal payments on your larger debts. Proceed to the next smallest debt after the smallest has been settled. This approach creates momentum and yields positive psychological effects.

- **Avalanche Technique:** Make the minimum payments on obligations with lower interest rates while giving priority to bills with the highest interest rates. This approach can be more economical and reduces the overall interest paid over time.

Debt Repayment Plan Creation:
- **Budget Allocation:** Set aside a certain amount of your income for debt repayment. Make debt repayments a priority in your monthly spending plan to make sure you are constantly making progress towards debt reduction.

- **Modifying Outlays:** Determine where you may make discretionary expenditure reductions to free up more money for debt repayment. Making changes to your spending plan will hasten the process of becoming debt-free.

3. Reaching an Agreement with Debtors

Reaching Out to Debtors:
- **Transparent Communication:** Speak with your creditors about your financial circumstances and look into ways to lower interest rates or payments. Depending on your situation, creditors might provide you with a modified payment plan or temporary reprieve.

- **Asking for Reduced Interest Rates:** Ask for a reduced interest rate on your loans or credit cards. A lower interest rate can shorten the length of your debt and hasten the payback process.

Looking Into Debt Reduction Options:
- **Consolidating Debt:** Take into consideration combining several loans into one with a reduced interest rate. Consolidating debt can lower the total amount of interest paid while streamlining payments. Make sure

consolidation loans have favourable terms by thoroughly evaluating them.

- Repayment of Debt: It can be possible in some circumstances to negotiate a debt settlement with creditors. Negotiating a lump-sum payment that is less than the entire amount owed is the process of debt settlement. Use caution because this strategy may have a negative effect on your credit score.

4. Prudent Credit Card Management

Managing Credit Wisely:
- Reducing Amounts Owed: To avoid accruing interest, try to pay off your credit card debt in full each month. Make more than the minimum payment if you are unable to pay the entire amount in order to pay off your debt more quickly.

- Resisting Take-On Debt: Avoid making new purchases using credit cards while you're trying to pay off previous debt. Refraining from taking on new debt can help you keep your finances from getting worse.

Create Positive Credit Habits:

- **Timely Payments:** Pay your bills on schedule to prevent late fines and credit score loss. Establish automated payments or reminders to make sure you never forget a deadline.

- **Keeping an Eye on Credit Utilisation:** Aim to use no more than 30% of your available credit as your credit utilisation ratio. Excessive credit utilisation may be a sign of impending financial strain and have a negative effect on your credit score.

5. Managing Student Debt

Knowing the Types of Loans:

- **Private vs. Federal Loans:** Distinguish between student loans that are provided by private and federal sources. When compared to private loans, federal loans frequently provide more flexible repayment options and possible forgiveness programs.

- Payback Schedules: Examine various federal student loan repayment options, including Graduated Repayment Plans and Income-Driven Repayment Plans (IDR). Select a strategy that fits your goals and financial circumstances.

Refinancing and Forgiveness:

- Loan Forgiveness Programs: Examine your eligibility for loan forgiveness initiatives like PSLF (Public Service Loan Forgiveness). Under certain circumstances, these programs can lower or eliminate outstanding loan balances.

- Options for refinancing: To get a better interest rate, think about refinancing your student loans. Refinancing may result in the loss of some advantages or safeguards but can also lower monthly payments and overall interest.

6. Managing Debt from Mortgages

Mortgage Management:
- **Refinancing:** Examine your alternatives if you want to refinance your mortgage to get better terms or a cheaper interest rate. You can lower your monthly payments and total interest expenses by refinancing.

- **Additional Payments:** Reduce the overall amount of interest paid and shorten the loan term by making additional principal payments towards your mortgage. Over time, even modest additional payments might make a big difference.

Attention to Home Equity:
- **Loans for Home Equity:** Consider a home equity loan or line of credit for substantial expenses or debt consolidation if you have a sizable amount of equity in your house. Take caution when using these solutions as they will raise your mortgage burden.

7. Developing Resilience in Finance

Emergency Fund:

- **Building a Safety Net:** Establish and keep an emergency fund to pay for unforeseen costs. Having an emergency fund helps you avoid having to use loans or credit cards in times of need.

- **Regular Savings:** Make consistent contributions to your emergency fund to keep it sufficiently funded. Aim to have three to six months' worth of living expenses set aside for emergencies.

Education in Finance:

- **Ongoing Education:** Spend time learning about finance to improve your knowledge of budgeting and debt management. Gaining knowledge enables you to make wise choices and enhance your financial circumstances.

- **Looking for Expert Guidance:** For individualised advice on debt management and enhancing your financial well-being, speak with credit counsellors or financial consultants. Expert counsel can offer insightful tips and useful tactics.

8. Sustaining Financial Well-Being Over Time

Determining Your Finances:
- **Short-Term Objectives:** Establish short-term financial objectives, including paying off particular debts or lowering credit card balances. Reaching short-term objectives increases momentum and confidence.

- **Long-Term Objectives:** Set long-term financial objectives, like home ownership or retirement savings. Match these objectives with your debt management strategy to guarantee a well-rounded financial strategy.

Monitoring Progress:
- **Regular Reviews:** Review your financial situation and debt payback status on a regular basis. If your income, expenses, or financial objectives change, make the necessary adjustments to your strategy.

- **Rejoicing in Achievement:** Celebrate and recognise your debt repayment accomplishments. Acknowledging successes encourages continued improvement and fosters sound financial practices.

Attaining financial independence and preserving general financial health depend on efficient debt management. You can try to reduce and eliminate debt by being aware of it, making repayment a priority, negotiating with creditors, and using credit prudently. Tailored techniques and meticulous planning are needed to handle some debt kinds, such mortgages and school loans.

Your financial stability is further improved by enhancing your financial resilience through professional counsel, emergency savings, and ongoing education. Managing debt becomes a manageable and satisfying endeavour with a systematic approach and commitment to financial health, setting the path for a safe and prosperous financial future.

➢ Methods for Collaborative Debt Relief

In order to effectively manage and pay off debt, a couple must work together, communicate, and share a commitment to sound financial management. Couples who collaborate can make the most of their joint resources and help one another become debt-free. The following are practical methods for combining debt repayment:

1. Honest Communication

Talk About Your Financial Situation:
- **Transparency and Honesty:** Talk about your individual and shared debts in an honest and transparent manner to start. Provide information about each debt, such as its total amount, interest rate, and monthly payment schedule.

- **Agreeing on Objectives:** Establish shared financial objectives and rank the debts that need to be paid off first. Establishing and talking about shared objectives makes sure that both parties are driven and in sync.

Consistent Check-Ins:
- **Monthly Get-togethers:** Set up frequent financial meetings to discuss the status of your debt payments. Talk about any difficulties or modifications to your financial situation, and modify your plans as necessary.

- **Help and Responsibility:** Take use of this chance to uplift and motivate one another throughout these gatherings. Honour accomplishments and work together to overcome any challenges.

2. Create a Collaboration Budget

Establish a Complete Budget:
- **Combash Funds:** Create a shared budget that accounts for all revenue and out-of-pocket costs. Set aside money

for savings, debt payments, and other important expenses.

- **Monitor Expenses:** To make sure you stick to your budget, keep an eye on your expenditures. Track your spending and find places where you may make savings by using apps or tools for budgeting.

Set Aside Money for Debt Repayment:
- **Rank Debt Payments:** Make sure that a sizable amount of your income is set aside in your budget for debt repayment. Repayment strategies that prioritise high-interest loans or those with the lowest balances should be followed.

- **Modify as Required:** Maintain flexibility in your budget by adjusting it in response to shifts in your income or expenses. To stay on track, reallocate money towards debt payments as needed.

3. Select a Plan for Repayment

Snowball Debt Method:

- Pay Attention to the Smallest Debts: Pay off the smallest debt first and make minimum payments on greater bills by using the debt snowball method. Proceed to the next smallest debt after the smallest has been settled.

- Gain Speed: As you observe success, this strategy gives you psychological rewards and encourages you to keep paying off debt.

Debt Avalanche Method:

- High-Interest Debts Should Be Prioritised: As an alternative, concentrate on the loans with the highest interest rates first and apply the debt avalanche technique. While focussing on the high-interest obligation, make the bare minimum payments on your other debts.

- Reduce Interest: By using this method, you can lower your overall debt faster and save money on interest.

Combined Strategies:

- **Hybrid Approach:** Certain couples opt for a hybrid strategy that incorporates aspects of both the avalanche and snowball approaches. For fast gains, pay off a few modest obligations and allocate additional income to high-interest debts.

4. Refinance and Consolidate

Combining Debts:

- **Debt Consolidation:** Take into consideration combining several debts into one lower-interest loan or credit card. This can make payments easier for you and possibly lower the total amount of interest you pay.

- **Score Choices:** To locate the best consolidation option for your case, thoroughly investigate your options and compare terms and interest rates.

Reduced Interest Rates:

- **Refinancing:** Refinance credit cards or high-interest loans to get a reduced interest rate. Over time, refinancing might result in lower monthly payments and interest savings.

- Verify Terms: Make sure any refinancing offers have favourable terms and don't include any additional fees or penalties by carefully reading the details.

5. Payment Automation

Avoid Late Fees:

- Set Up Automatic Payments: To guarantee that debt payments are made on schedule each month, automate them. To prevent late fines and possible harm to your credit score, set up automatic transfers from your bank account to your creditors.

- Coherence: Automating payments lowers the possibility of missed payments and promotes consistency. It also makes managing your finances easier.

Increase Payments:

- **Modify Payment Amounts:** If things become better financially, you might want to think about raising your automatic payments in order to pay off debt faster. You can lower interest expenses and pay off debt faster by making additional payments.

6. Establish an Emergencies Fund

Build a Safety Net:
- **Save for Emergencies:** Set up an emergency fund to pay for unforeseen costs and stop more debt from accruing. Having an emergency fund lessens the need to use credit cards or loans in times of need by acting as a buffer.

- **Refund Often:** Regularly add to your emergency fund with the goal of having three to six months' worth of living expenses there. Adapt contributions to your spending plan and financial objectives.

Never Use Credit for Emergencies:

- Instead, Use Savings: When unanticipated costs arise, pay them using your emergency money rather than using credit cards or loans. This keeps you on track with your payback schedule and helps stop additional debt accumulation.

7. Get Expert Assistance

Money Guidance:
- Expert Consultation: Consider getting assistance from a financial expert or counsellor if managing debt becomes too much for you to handle. Experts can offer advice on financial planning, budgeting, and debt repayment techniques.

- Plans for Managing Debt: You might draft a debt management plan (DMP) with the assistance of a financial counsellor, which lays out an organised strategy for paying off your obligations. DMPs may provide consolidated payments and reduced interest rates.

Credit Guidance:

- **Credit Enhancement:** Services for credit counselling might help you manage your debt and raise your credit score. They provide tools and information to assist you in creating better financial practices and plans.

8. Keep an Upbeat Attitude

Remain Inspired:
- **Remember to Celebrate Every Milestone:** Honour every debt payback achievement, no matter how minor. Acknowledging your progress helps you stay motivated and reinforces good behaviour.

- **Help One Another Out:** Throughout the debt payback process, provide each other moral support and encouragement. Sustaining motivation and tenacity is facilitated by keeping an optimistic outlook.

Aim for Long-Term Objectives:
- **Credit Independence:** Remember your long-term financial objectives, such becoming financially independent, building retirement funds, or buying a

house. Maintaining concentration on these objectives gives direction and drive.

Adjust and Modify:
- **Be Adaptable:** Be ready to modify your tactics and approach in response to evolving conditions. Being flexible enables you to deal with unforeseen obstacles and maintain your debt repayment plan.

As a partnership, you need to be committed, cooperative, and methodical in your debt repayment. Couples can effectively manage and reduce debt by having open lines of communication, creating a common budget, selecting efficient repayment plans, and getting expert assistance when necessary.

Creating an emergency fund, setting up automatic payments, and keeping an optimistic outlook all help one become financially independent and healthy. Couples can successfully walk the route to debt freedom and establish a solid financial foundation for the future with commitment and cooperation.

➢ Reducing Credit and Keeping Off New Debt

Paying off current debts, preventing the accrual of new debt, and keeping a clean credit report are all necessary for effectively managing debt and establishing financial security as a partnership. Achieving financial independence and maintaining long-term financial health require effective credit management and debt avoidance measures. Here's a thorough explanation on how to safely manage your credit and stay out of debt:

1. Formulating a Financial Plan and Budget

Create a Reasonable Budget:
- **Monitor Revenue and Expenses:** Make a thorough budget that lists all of your revenue and cost sources. This will assist you in determining where you can make savings and budget money for other financial objectives, such as paying off debt.

- Give Needs More Weight Than Wants: Make a distinction between expenditure that is necessary and that which is optional. Prioritise paying off debt and purchasing needs before making purchases of non-essentials.

Prepare for Future Costs:
- Emergency Fund: Establish and keep an emergency fund to pay for unforeseen costs. In times of need, having a safety net prevents you from depending too much on loans or credit cards.

- Dying Money: Establish sinking accounts for anticipated future costs, including big-ticket items, home maintenance, or vacations. Make consistent contributions to these funds to prevent taking on additional debt to cover these costs.

2. Making Responsible Use of Credit

Comprehend Terms of Credit:

- **Aware of Your Credit Limits:** Keep an eye on your credit card limits and refrain from using them all at once. Your credit score can be raised by keeping your credit utilisation ratio—the ratio of the amount of credit you utilise to your credit limit—low.

- **Be Aware of Interest Rates:** Recognise the interest rates on the credit accounts you own. Elevated interest rates have the potential to escalate borrowing expenses and complicate debt repayment.

Make On Time Payments:

- **Avoid Late Fees:** Make sure you pay off all of your loans and credit card balances on schedule. To help you remember to make your payments on time and save late fees, set up automatic payments or reminders.

- **Pay Above the Minimum Amount:** Paying more than the minimal amount will help you pay off your bill more quickly and save money on interest. Whenever you pay off your balance in full each month, interest is not charged.

3. Steer clear of pointless credit applications

Restrict Credit Enquiries:
- Apply Selectively: Applying for new credit accounts should only be done when absolutely necessary. Regular credit enquiries may indicate possible financial instability and have a negative effect on your credit score.

- View Your Credit Report Here: Examine your credit report on a regular basis to ensure accuracy and to learn about your credit status. To make sure all the information is accurate, request a free credit report once a year from the major credit bureaus.

Be Aware of the Effects of New Credit:
- Take Your Credit Score Into Account: Due to rigorous enquiries, obtaining new credit may momentarily reduce your credit score. Determine whether getting a new credit account is in line with your credit management plan and financial objectives.

- **Evaluate Your Credit Needs:** Consider if obtaining fresh credit is really necessary before applying. Think about if a new credit account offers substantial advantages or if you can accomplish your objectives with your current credit accounts.

4. Prudent Credit Management

- **Keep Your Credit Utilisation Under Check:** Keep your credit card balances far below your credit limitations in order to Maintain a Good Credit Score. Your credit score is positively impacted by a reduced credit use ratio.

- **Spread Out Credit Categories:** Your credit score can be improved by having a variety of credit kinds, such as installment loans and credit cards. Make sure you handle each credit kind sensibly.

Address Credit Issues Promptly:
- **Resolve Discrepancies:**** If you discover any errors or inconsistencies on your credit report, get in touch with

the credit bureau and submit the required paperwork as soon as possible.

- Control Past Due Dates: Make contact with your creditors to talk about possibilities like payment plans or temporary relief if you run into financial issues that interfere with your capacity to make payments.

5. Getting Knowledge for Both You and Your Spouse

Education in Finances:
- Remain Up to Date: Learn about credit management, debt payback plans, and financial planning for both you and your spouse. Having a solid understanding of financial principles and best practices enables you to make wise choices.

- Participate in workshops: Take part in webinars, counselling sessions, or courses on financial literacy to learn how to prevent debt and manage your credit well.

Agree on Financial Goals:

- **Determine Specific Goals:** As a couple, decide on financial objectives including debt freedom, emergency fund building, and down payment savings for a home. Working together and coordinating your goals will improve your financial partnership.

- **Monitor Status:** Review your financial status on a regular basis and make any necessary adjustments to your plan. Reevaluate objectives and recognise accomplishments to keep yourself inspired and concentrated on reaching financial freedom.

6. Credit Development and Preservation

Building a Credit Record:
- **Get Started Early:** If you don't have any credit history, think about opening an account with a secured credit card or adding yourself as an authorised user to someone else's account. Having a good credit history from an early age can help you later on.

- **Apply Credit Wisely:** By utilising credit accounts sensibly, making timely bill payments, and avoiding high credit utilisation, you can preserve a good credit history.

Keeping Old Accounts Open:
- **Maintaining Good Credit Habits:** To extend the duration of your credit history, hold onto older credit accounts with a good payment record. Your credit score may be impacted negatively by closing previous accounts.

- **Continually Review Credit:** To keep track of your credit health, monitor your credit reports and scores on a regular basis. To keep your credit profile strong, take quick action on any difficulties.

Achieving financial independence as a partnership requires both of you to refrain from taking on additional debt and to handle credit responsibly. Couples can establish a strong financial foundation and work towards their long-term financial objectives by making a realistic budget, using credit responsibly, avoiding pointless credit applications, and maintaining a high credit score.

Your financial relationship will be strengthened and a successful path to financial independence will be supported by educating yourselves and establishing clear financial goals. You and your partner may accomplish your shared financial goals and find financial stability with dedication, cooperation, and well-informed decision-making.

➢ Establishing an Emergencies Fund

A vital component of financial stability and security is an emergency fund, which acts as a safety net in case of unanticipated circumstances like major repairs, job loss, or medical issues. Creating and keeping an emergency fund guarantees that you and your spouse are ready for unforeseen costs and helps avoid financial stress. This is a thorough tutorial on creating a successful emergency fund:

1. Realising How Critical an Emergency Fund Is

Intention and Advantages:
- **Money Safety Net:** An emergency reserve acts as a safety net to absorb unforeseen costs without upsetting your financial objectives. It lessens the reliance on loans and credit cards, which can result in debt accumulation.

- **Peace of Mind:** Feeling secure in the knowledge that you have an emergency money on hand eases your mind and eases your financial concern.

Types of Emergencies Covered:
- **Medical Emergencies:** Unexpected medical bills or health conditions that demand rapid attention.

- **Job Loss:** A brief reduction in income as a result of underemployment or unemployment.

- **house Repairs:** Unexpected costs associated with house upkeep, such as a broken furnace or a leaky roof. -

- **Vehicle Repairs:** Unexpected costs associated with auto maintenance or repairs.

2. Calculating How Much to Put in Your Emergency Fund

Monetarily Estimate Your Outlays:
- **Keep Track of Your Spending:** Examine your monthly spending on groceries, utilities, insurance, rent or a mortgage, and transportation. This can assist you in figuring out how much money is required to pay for necessities.

- **Assess the Fund Amount:** Aim for three to six months' worth of living expenses as a basic guideline. This gives you enough wiggle room to handle unexpected costs without using credit.

Take Into Account Your Particular Situation:

- **Income Stability:** If your income is steady and your work is secure, a modest emergency fund (about three months' worth of costs) might be enough. On the other hand, go for a larger fund (six months or more) if your income is erratic.

- **Dependents and Obligations:** Take into account the total number of dependents as well as any additional debts you may have. Families with more obligations or kids could require a bigger emergency reserve.

3. Establishing and Keeping Up Your Emergency Savings

Select an account to save money:
- **High-Yield Savings Accounts:** To optimise interest on your emergency fund, choose a money market account or a high-yield savings account. These accounts yield higher returns than regular savings accounts.

- **Compatibility:** Make sure you have easy access to your emergency savings without sacrificing convenience. Refrain from storing cash in accounts that can entice you to use it for non-urgent expenses.

Contributions from Autonomy:

- Configure Transfers Automatically: To guarantee steady savings, set up recurring monthly contributions to your emergency fund. Establish a direct deposit into your emergency fund account from your bank account.

- Modify Donations: To hasten the growth of your fund, modify the amount you contribute as your financial circumstances change (e.g., a rise in pay, a decrease in spending).

- Keep an eye on the fund and make regular reviews: Make sure your emergency money is still sufficient for your needs by periodically reviewing it. As your costs or financial circumstances change, adjust the size of the fund.

- **Refuel As Required:** Prioritise reloading your emergency reserve as soon as you can if you must spend funds from it in order to preserve your financial stability.

4. Methods for Increasing Your Emergency Savings

Begin Small:

- **Establish Gradual Objectives:** Start with a modest, doable goal, like saving $500 or $1,000. After you meet this objective, progressively raise your goal until you reach the required quantity.

- **Celebrate Milestones:** To maintain your motivation and dedication to increasing your emergency fund, mark and commemorate significant junctures along your savings path.

Reduce Superfluous Expenses:

- **Assess Your Budget:** Determine which non-essential costs can be cut or eliminated. Put the money you save by cutting these costs back into an emergency fund.

- **Make savings a priority:** Consider the contributions you make to your emergency fund as a fixed item in your spending plan. Set aside money for savings before making purchases of luxuries.

Boost Revenue:
- **Discover Side Jobs:** Take into Account Adding Extra Revenue Sources: Take into Account Taking on Part-Time Jobs, Freelance Work, or Gig Economy Opportunities. Boost your emergency savings with this additional revenue.

- **Assign Windfalls:** Your emergency fund will grow more quickly if you put any unforeseen financial windfalls—such as tax returns, bonuses, or gifts—toward it.

5. Steer Clear of Typical Pitfalls

Avoid Using Emergency Funds for Non-Emergencies:
- **Strict Definition:** Specify what an emergency is in order to protect the fund from being used for non-urgent

costs. Remember to reserve the fund for actual emergencies only.

- Observation Withdrawals: Keep track of all your emergency fund withdrawals and make sure they correspond with the emergencies you have designated. Review your expenditures frequently to prevent making needless withdrawals.

Keep Up Regular Contributions:
- Don't Ignore the Fund: Refrain from cutting back on or skipping payments to your emergency fund, especially when things are tight financially. Regular contributions are essential to the fund's creation and upkeep.

- Replenish Quickly: To guarantee ongoing financial security, if you must utilise the emergency fund, give it first priority to be restored as quickly as you can.

6. Adjusting to Shifts in Life

Adjusting Fund Size:

- **Life Events:** Significant life events, including starting a family, purchasing a property, or switching careers, may require adjusting the amount in your emergency fund. Reassess your requirements and modify the fund if necessary.

- **Income Changes:** Notable adjustments to your income, including a rise or decrease, may affect your capacity to make contributions to the fund. In light of your changed financial circumstances, modify your contributions.

Timely Evaluations and Reports:
- **Semiannual Evaluations:** Plan to have your emergency fund and general financial status reviewed on a frequent basis. As necessary, make changes to the fund to make sure it still meets your needs and offers sufficient security.

One of the most important steps towards obtaining financial independence and security as a marriage is setting up an emergency fund. You may build a strong safety net to handle unforeseen expenses by figuring out the right amount, opening a specific savings account, automating contributions, and avoiding typical errors and mistakes. Making your emergency fund a priority and keeping it up to date will ease your mind and shield you from financial strain in the event of unanticipated circumstances. You and your partner may make sure you are well-prepared for life's uncertainties and keep moving towards success and financial stability with persistent effort and thoughtful planning.

Chapter Five

Tax Planning and Efficiency

One of the most important components of financial management that can have a big impact on your overall financial health is tax planning and optimisation. Developing a strategy to reduce your tax liability while adhering to tax laws and regulations is a necessary component of effective tax planning. A detailed study of tax rules, possible credits, deductions, and tax benefit optimisation techniques is necessary for this process. This thorough tax planning and optimisation guide will assist you and your partner in creating and preserving financial security.

1. Getting the Hang of Tax Planning

- Definition and Goals of Tax Planning: The process of organising your financial affairs to reduce your tax liability and maximise your tax benefits is known as tax planning. To maximise your tax situation, it entails making well-informed judgements regarding income, investments, and spending.

- Time and Approach: Proactive thinking and intelligent decision-making are necessary for effective tax planning. It's more important to manage your finances to make sure you pay the minimum amount necessary by law than it is to avoid paying taxes.

The Significance of Tax Planning:
- Minimising Tax Liability: You can lower your tax liability by carefully controlling your income and out-of-pocket spending. Over time, this can result in considerable savings.

- Improving Economic Effectiveness: In order to achieve your financial objectives while minimising tax implications, tax planning helps you optimise your financial strategy, including retirement planning and investment choices.

2. Important Tax Planning Elements

Knowing Your Tax Brackets:

- **Progressive Tax System:** The majority of tax systems are progressive in nature, meaning that higher income brackets are subject to increasing rates of taxation. You can minimise your taxable income by planning your income and deductions based on your understanding of tax bands.

- **Income Management:** You can avoid paying more in taxes by strategically controlling your income, such as by delaying income or timing the receipt of bonuses.

Itemised Deductions:

- **Maximising Deductions and Credits:** You can itemise certain expenses, such as property taxes, mortgage interest, and charity contributions, to lower your taxable income. Keep a record of these costs all year long.

- **Credits for Taxes:** Your tax liability is directly decreased by tax credits. Credits for child care costs, energy-efficient home upgrades, and school expenses are a few examples. Make sure you understand the qualifications for each credit that is available, as well as all of them.

Retirement Accounts:

- **Tax-Advantaged Accounts:** There may be tax advantages to making contributions to retirement accounts that are tax-advantaged, such 401(k)s and IRAs. While contributions to Roth IRAs are made with after-tax money and enable tax-free withdrawals in retirement, donations to standard retirement accounts are frequently tax deductible.

- **HSAs (Health Savings Accounts):** HSAs provide three tax advantages: tax-deductible contributions, tax-free account growth, and tax-free withdrawals for approved medical costs.

3. Tax optimisation and investment strategies

Investments with Low Taxes:

- **Capital Gains and Losses:** Knowing the tax implications of investments, such as short-term versus long-term capital gains, can help you make the most of your investing plan. Tax rates on long-term capital gains are often lower than those on short-term gains.

- **Investments Free From Taxes:** Take into account investments like municipal bonds that provide income that is tax-exempt. Generally speaking, interest on these bonds is not subject to federal income tax.

Offsetting Gains:

- **Tax-Loss Harvesting:** Selling investments that have lost value is a way to counteract capital gains from other investments. You can lower your entire tax obligation by using this method.

- **Readjusting:** Rebalancing your portfolio on a regular basis can help you realise gains and losses in a way that minimises your tax liability and ensures that your investment plan is in line with your financial objectives.

Investments and Retirement Accounts:

- **Tax-Efficient Withdrawals:** Strategically plan retirement account withdrawals to reduce taxes. For instance, you can lower your overall tax burden by taking withdrawals from taxable accounts before tax-advantaged accounts.

- **Minimum Mandatory Distributions (RMDs):** Recognise the RMD regulations for traditional retirement funds in order to prevent penalties and efficiently handle your tax liability.

4. Couples Tax Planning

Separate vs. Joint Filing:
- **Combining Income and Deductions:** Ascertain which filing method will result in the most tax savings—joint or separate. While filing jointly frequently opens up greater tax benefits, there are some circumstances in which filing separately may be preferable.

- **Dividing Up Income:** Investigate income splitting tactics to lower your total tax obligation. To maximise tax brackets and deductions, for instance, transferring assets or income between spouses may be helpful.

Common Financial Objectives and Tax Consequences:

- **Organising Financial Decisions:** Work together on financial decisions that have an effect on taxes, like significant purchases, retirement planning, and investment selections. By coordinating these choices, you can maximise tax advantages and accomplish common financial objectives.

- **Family Tax Planning Considerations:** Take into account the tax ramifications of family-related issues, including estate planning, dependent care, and educational costs. Plan to maximise tax advantages and efficiently handle financial obligations.

5. Handling Tax Updates and Modifications

Remaining Up to Date:

- Changes in Tax Laws: Tax rules and regulations are subject to periodic changes that affect tax rates, credits, and deductions. Keep yourself updated on any developments that can impact your tax preparation techniques.

- Professionals Offering Consultation: Engage in collaboration with tax experts or financial counsellors to remain current on modifications to tax legislation and obtain customised guidance based on your financial circumstances.

Modifying Approaches:

- Adjusting to New Regulations: Adapt your tax planning techniques to new tax legislation, changes in your financial situation, or life events. Make sure your tax plan is still appropriate and compliant by reviewing and updating it on a regular basis.

- Examining Tax Returns: Every year, check your tax returns for correctness and look for areas where you can optimise them. Correct any inconsistencies or mistakes right away to prevent future problems with the tax authorities.

6. Resources and Tools for Tax Planning

Software and App Utilisation:

- **Tax Preparation Software:** Utilise tax preparation software to find possible credits and deductions and to expedite the tax filing process. You may maximise your tax benefits by using the optimisation tools and assistance provided by several software alternatives.

- **Apps for Financial Planning:** To keep tabs on investments, manage spending, and prepare taxes, use financial planning applications. These resources might offer perceptions and suggestions for improving your financial circumstances.

Seeking Professional Advice:

- **Tax consultants:** Seek professional advice on sophisticated tax matters, such as company income, investment strategies, and estate planning, from tax consultants or accountants.

- Money Management: To create a thorough tax planning approach that complements your entire financial goals and objectives, collaborate with financial planners.

Achieving long-term financial success and managing your finances effectively depend on efficient tax planning and optimisation. You can create a plan to reduce your tax payment and optimise benefits by learning about important elements such as tax brackets, deductions, credits, and tax-advantaged accounts.

Coordination of financial decisions and joint tax strategy optimisation can improve financial stability and assist in achieving common objectives for couples. You may effectively manage the complexity of tax preparation by using tools and resources, staying up to date on tax developments, and getting professional counsel. You may improve your overall financial well-being and maximise your tax situation with proactive management and cautious preparation.

➢ Filing Taxes Jointly vs. Separately

One of the first choices you'll have to make when filing taxes together is whether to file jointly or separately. Your financial status, tax liability, and eligibility for certain credits and deductions can all be greatly impacted by this decision. Making an educated choice that supports your financial objectives can be facilitated by being aware of the benefits, drawbacks, and factors to take into account for each alternative.

1. Joint Filing: Advantages and Benefits

Higher Standard Deduction:
- **Increased Tax Benefits:** When filing jointly, couples are frequently eligible for a larger standard deduction than when filing individually. The standard deduction for

married couples filing jointly for the 2024 tax year is $27,700, while the standard deduction for single taxpayers filing separately is $13,850.

- Qualification for Credits: You may be able to claim a number of tax credits and deductions if you file jointly that you would not be able to claim if you file separately. These consist of education-related credits like the American Opportunity Credit, the Child and Dependent Care Credit, and the Earned Income Tax Credit (EITC).

Benefits of the Tax Bracket:
- Lower Tax Rates: In general, filing jointly gives you access to more advantageous tax brackets. For joint filers, the income limits for tax brackets are frequently higher, which may lead to a lower effective tax rate and a smaller total tax burden.

Single Tax Return:
- Simplified Filing: Filing jointly streamlines the process and lowers the possibility of error by requiring the submission of just one tax return. When compared to

filing separately, it might also be simpler to handle and require less time.

Increased Deduction Allowances:
- **Phase-Out Ceilings:** There are income-based phase-out levels for a number of credits and deductions. In addition to the enhanced tax benefits, filing jointly frequently permits larger income limitations prior to the phase-out of these credits and deductions.

2. Separate Filing: Benefits and Drawbacks

Achievable Gains:
- **Dividing Up Debts:** In terms of tax obligations, filing separately can offer some separation. Filing separately can shield the other spouse from joint liabilities if one spouse has serious tax problems or is facing penalties.

- **Personal Withdrawals:** When filing separately, a spouse may occasionally be able to claim credits or deductions that would not be accessible or limited when filing jointly. For instance, if one spouse has high medical costs, they may be able to claim a higher tax deduction if their income is lower.

Drawbacks:
- **Higher Tax Rates:** Separate filing frequently results in lower access to tax brackets and higher tax rates. When compared to filing jointly, this may result in a larger overall tax liability.

- **Reductions and Losses of Credits:** Couples filing separately are not eligible for a number of tax perks and deductions. This can lead to a greater tax payment and includes the Earned Income Tax Credit (EITC), Child and Dependent Care Credit, and education credits.

- **Difficult Mathematical Operations:** Certain credits and deductions may be more difficult to calculate if separate filing is made. For instance, dividing itemised deductions between couples may produce less advantageous results than filing jointly.

3. Taking into Accounts to Select the Optimal Filing Status

Differences in Income:

- Inequalities in Income Levels: Filing jointly may provide tax benefits if one spouse earns much more than the other because lower tax brackets and greater income limits can be used. On the other hand, filing separately may help to optimise benefits if one spouse has significant credits or deductions.

Deductions and Credits:

- Itemised Deductions: Examine which offers a greater tax benefit: using the standard deduction or itemised deductions. Filing jointly may maximise deductions for couples with sizable itemised expenses, such as mortgage interest, real estate taxes, or medical costs.

- Credits Are Available: Based on your filing status, determine your eligibility for tax credits and deductions. A broader range of credits and deductions are frequently available when filing jointly, which may lower total tax burden.

Financial and Legal Repercussions:
- **Shared Liability:** When filing jointly, the accuracy of the tax return and any associated liabilities are equally the responsibility of both spouses. Think about the costs associated with joint liability and if they match your financial objectives and situation.

- **Attention to State Taxes:** There may be differences in state tax rules and regulations about filing jointly or individually. To understand how state tax rules may affect your choice, think about how state taxes affect your total tax status and speak with a tax specialist.

Repercussions in the Future:
- **Elong-Term Effect:** Consider the potential effects of your filing status on your long-term financial objectives. Whether filing jointly or individually depends on a number of considerations, including future financial goals, estate preparation, and retirement planning.

4. Making the Choice: Doable Actions

Examine Your Cash Position:
- **Compute and Evaluate:** Your tax liability under both filing statuses can be computed using tax software or by speaking with a tax expert. To ascertain which choice offers the greatest overall tax benefit, compare the outcomes.

- **Assess Your Objectives:** When selecting the optimal file status, consider your financial objectives, obligations, and prospective advantages. Think about how filing separately or jointly fits into your long-term financial goals.

Speak with a Tax Professional:
- **Seek Expert Advice:** Speak with a financial advisor or tax professional to receive recommendations and insights tailored to your unique financial circumstances. They can offer advice on how to make wise choices and maximise your tax plan.

Annual Review:

- Annual Evaluation: Every year, check that your filing status still reflects your goals and financial circumstances. The ideal filing status for your circumstances may change depending on your income, deductions, or life circumstances.

For couples, whether to file jointly or individually can have a significant impact on their overall tax liability and financial status. File separately if you want to maximise your individual deductions or shield one spouse from joint liabilities, even though filing jointly sometimes offers more advantageous tax benefits and credits. You can make an informed decision that supports your financial objectives and improves your overall financial well-being by examining your financial status, taking into account potential tax implications, and consulting a specialist.

➢ Tax-Efficient Investing: Techniques to Reduce Liabilities and Increase Returns

Choosing and managing investments to reduce tax obligations and increase after-tax profits is known as tax-efficient investing. Good tax preparation while investing can make a big difference in your overall wealth accumulation and financial progress. Making decisions that are in line with your financial objectives can be facilitated by having a thorough understanding of the many tax-efficient investment and strategy options.

1. Gaining Knowledge About Tax-Efficient Investing

Idea and Significance:
- **Tax Effectiveness:** Tax-efficient investing aims to reduce the effect of taxes on your capital gains and investment income in order to optimise after-tax profits. Since taxes have the potential to reduce investment returns, long-term growth optimisation requires careful tax planning.

- Effect on Refunds: Dividends, interest, and capital gains taxes are examples of investment income that can have a big impact on overall returns. Tax-efficient solutions can help you pay less in taxes while increasing the potential for your investments to grow.

- Capital Gains Tax: The tax on the profit received by selling an asset, like stocks or real estate, is known as the Capital Gains Tax. The tax rate on long-term capital gains—those derived from assets held for more than a year—is typically lower than the tax rate on short-term capital gains.

- Dividend Tax: Income taxed on dividends earned from mutual funds or equities. Dividends that meet certain requirements are taxed differently than regular dividends.

- Interest Income Tax: This is a tax on interest received from bonds, savings accounts, and other investments that yield interest. Generally, interest income is subject to ordinary income tax rates.

2. Investment Strategies That Save Taxes

Make use of tax-advantaged accounts:

- **IRAs, or Individual Retirement Accounts:** Traditional IRA contributions are tax deductible, and the growth of the investments is tax-deferred until withdrawal. Roth IRAs offer substantial tax advantages by allowing tax-free withdrawals on qualifying distributions.

- **HSAs (Health Savings Accounts):** Tax deductions are available for contributions to HSAs, and withdrawals used for approved medical costs are tax-free. Growth on investments made inside an HSA is likewise tax-free.

Invest in Tax-Efficient Funds:

- **Index Funds and ETFs:** Compared to actively managed funds, index funds and ETFs often have lower turnover rates, which means fewer taxable events and smaller capital gains distributions.

- **Mutual Funds with Tax Efficiency:** Certain mutual funds are expressly made to use techniques like tax-loss harvesting and reducing high-turnover trades in order to reduce taxable dividends as much as possible.

Use Tax-Loss Harvesting:
- **Offset Gains with Losses:** Using tax-loss harvesting, investments are sold at a loss in order to deduct capital gains from other investments. By using this method, you may be able to minimise your total tax obligation as well as your taxable capital gains.

- **Rule for Wash Sales:** Keep in mind the wash sale rule, which states that if you repurchase the identical security within 30 days following the sale, you cannot deduct your loss. Consider getting a comparable but distinct security to avoid this.

Maximise Asset Allocation:
- **Accounts that are Taxable versus Tax-Advantaged:** Bonds and high-yield dividend stocks are examples of tax-inefficient investments. Put them in tax-advantaged

accounts where the income is protected from taxes. To take advantage of advantageous tax treatment, invest in tax-efficient products like index funds or exchange-traded funds (ETFs) in taxable accounts.

- **Bond Funds with Tax Efficiency:** Taxable accounts may benefit from the tax-free interest income that municipal bonds and municipal bond funds can provide.

Make Use of Tax-Sensible Investment Options:
- **City Bonds:** Municipal bond interest income is often free from state and local taxes as well as federal income tax. For high earners who want to receive money free of taxes, they may be a cost-effective choice.

- **Tax-Efficient Real Estate Investments:** Qualified dividend distributions from real estate investment trusts (REITs) can produce income that is tax-efficient. Tax advantages may also be obtained by purchasing real estate through tax-advantaged accounts.

3. Examples and Case Studies

Example 1: Tax-Loss Harvesting in Action

Scenario: Two equities are owned by an investor; Stock A has earned $5,000 while Stock B has lost $3,000. The investor can lower the taxable gain to $2,000 by offsetting $3,000 of the capital gains from Stock A by selling Stock B at a loss.

Result: A $3,000 reduction in the investor's taxable capital gains lowers their overall tax liability and increases after-tax returns.

Example 2: Asset Location Optimisation

Scenario: An investor has a tax-advantaged IRA in addition to a taxable account. They put their interest-bearing bond assets into the IRA in order to take advantage of tax-deferred growth. They take advantage of the advantageous capital gains tax treatment by placing their index funds in the taxable account.

Result: By reducing taxes on interest income and capital gains, the investor maximises tax efficiency and improves overall after-tax profits.

4. Possible Obstacles and Things to Take Into Account

Complexity and Management:

- **Complexity of Tax Planning:** Careful planning and continuous management are necessary for the implementation of tax-efficient techniques. Investors need to be up to date on tax rules and regulations so they may modify their plans as necessary.

- **Keeping Records:** For efficient tax planning and reporting, precise records of transactions, cost basis, and investment performance must be kept.

Modifications to Tax Laws:

- **Legislative Adjustments:** The efficacy of tax-efficient solutions is subject to change due to changes in tax laws and regulations. Keep abreast of modifications to tax laws and seek advice from a tax expert to modify your tactics.

Aligning Strategies with Goals:

- Personal Financial Goals: Make sure your investment objectives and overall financial goals are in line with tax-efficient practices. When putting tax-efficient investing methods into practice, take into account variables like risk tolerance, time horizon, and liquidity requirements.

Managing your investments and optimising after-tax earnings require tax-efficient investing. You can reduce your tax obligations and improve your total financial growth by learning and putting into practice tax-efficient tactics, such as using tax-advantaged accounts, investing in tax-efficient funds, and using tax-loss harvesting. You can successfully negotiate the difficulties of tax-efficient investment and meet your long-term financial objectives by remaining up to date on tax regulations, strategically placing your assets, and consulting a financial advisor.

➢ Understanding Tax Benefits for Partners: Optimising Economic Gains

Couples who jointly handle their finances might take advantage of a number of tax advantages to improve their overall financial position. A more effective tax plan and large savings might result from knowing these tax advantages and knowing how to use them. The main tax benefits for couples will be discussed in this part, along with filing options, credits, deductions, and methods for maximising these advantages.

1. Joint versus Separate Filing Status

1.1 Collaborative Filing:
- **Tax Brackets:** In general, filing jointly gives you access to more advantageous tax brackets. Higher income thresholds before higher tax rates apply to couples filing jointly, which may reduce their overall tax liability.

- **Normal Calculation:** The standard deduction for married couples filing jointly for the 2024 tax year is $27,700, while it is $13,850 for single filers. This increased deduction can save a significant amount of money by lowering taxable income.

- **Deductions and Credits for Taxes:** Couples who file jointly may be eligible for a number of tax credits and deductions that are either reduced or unavailable if they file separately. These consist of dependent care credits, education credits, and child tax credits.

1.2 Independent File Submission:
- **When It Makes Sense:** In certain circumstances, such as when one spouse has large medical costs or other deductions that surpass the itemisation level, filing separately may be advantageous. It may also be helpful if one spouse is enrolled in an income-driven repayment plan and has significant student loan debt.

- **Restrictions:** Couples filing separately may not be eligible for certain tax benefits, including the education credits and earned income tax credit (EITC). Furthermore, when compared to filing jointly, tax brackets and deductions are typically less advantageous.

2. Tax Credits and Deductions

2.1 Breakdown of Deductions:

- **Interest on Mortgage:** Mortgage interest on a couple's primary and secondary residences is deductible. Only interest on up to $750,000 in mortgage debt (or $375,000 for a married couple filing separately) may be deducted.

- **Local and State Taxes (SALT):** Couples can deduct up to $10,000 in combined state and local income taxes or property taxes under the SALT deduction.

- **Donations to Charities:** One way to lower taxable income is to make deductions for donations to approved charity organisations. To ensure proper reporting, make sure to maintain records of contributions.

2.2 Tax Credits:

- **Kid Tax Credit:** Couples may claim a credit of up to $2,000 for each eligible kid for the 2024 tax year. It's crucial to determine eligibility based on combined income because this credit phases out at higher income levels.

- **Earned Income Tax Credit (EITC):** Working couples with low to moderate incomes can receive financial aid from the EITC. The amount of the credit is determined on the number of dependents, filing status, and income.

- **Credits for Education:** Education costs may be partially mitigated by the American Opportunity Credit and Lifetime Learning Credit. To be eligible for these credits, couples must meet certain income and eligibility conditions.

3. Contributions to Retirement

3.1 Contributions to a Traditional IRA:
- **Tax Deduction:** Tax-deductible contributions to a regular IRA can lower taxable income. Couples may pay

up to $6,500 each person for 2024 ($7,500 if they are 50 years of age or older).

- **Average Income:** At higher income levels, the deductibility of IRA contributions may taper out, especially if one or both couples are enrolled in an employer-sponsored retirement plan.

3.2 Contributions to a Roth IRA:

- **Withdrawals Tax-Free:** After-tax money is used to fund a Roth IRA, but eligible withdrawals are tax-free. To contribute, a couple must fulfil the income qualifying conditions.

- **Limited Contributions:** The contribution cap for 2024 is $6,500 per individual ($7,500 if an individual is 50 years of age or older), with phase-out levels determined by modified adjusted gross income.

3.3 Plans Sponsored by Employers:

- **Contributions to 401(k) Plans:** Pre-tax money is used to fund 401(k) contributions, which lowers taxable income. The contribution cap for 2024 is $22,500 per individual ($30,000 for those over 50). To take advantage of employer matching and tax-deferred growth, couples should maximise their contributions.

4. Accounts for Health Savings (HSAs)

4.1 Benefits to Taxation:
- **Triple Tax Benefit:** Tax deductions are available for contributions made to an HSA; growth is tax-free; and withdrawals made for approved medical costs are tax-free. HSAs are an effective tool for controlling healthcare expenditures and setting money aside for future needs because of this triple tax benefit.

- **Limited Contributions:** Couples may contribute an HSA in 2024 up to $7,750 ($8,750 if they are 55 years of age or older). To fully benefit from the tax advantages, contributions must be made.

5. Planning for Estate and Gift Taxes

5.1 Exemption from Estate Tax:

- **Unified Credit:** Couples can avoid paying estate taxes on a combined amount of up to $25.84 million, since the federal estate tax exemption for individuals is $12.92 million in 2024. To optimise this exemption and lower inheritance tax obligations, proper estate planning is recommended.

- **Portability for Spouses:** In effect, spouses can double the inheritance tax exemption amount by transferring any unused share to their surviving spouse.

6. Couples' Tax Planning Techniques

6.1 Dividing Income:

- **Transferring Income:** To lower their total tax obligation, couples might divide their income between the two of them by using income-splitting techniques. This may entail making tax-efficient investment choices or modifying one's sources of income.

- **Managing Tax Brackets:** Couples can minimise their tax burden and remain in lower tax rates by strategically managing their income and deductions.

6.2 Aligning Strategies with Financial Objectives:

- Long-term financial objectives including debt management, retirement savings, and school funding should all be coordinated with tax preparation. A holistic approach to wealth management is ensured by coordinating tax tactics with financial objectives.

6.3 Seeking Expert Guidance:
- **Accounting Specialists:** Couples can maximise benefits, create a customised tax plan, and negotiate complex tax laws by speaking with a financial advisor or tax specialist. Expert guidance guarantees that tax planning is in line with personal objectives and circumstances.

To maximise savings and optimise financial results, couples must comprehend and take advantage of tax benefits. Couples can better manage their tax obligations and improve their financial situation by investigating filing alternatives, tax deductions, credits, retirement contributions, and estate planning. To optimise the advantages of tax-efficient solutions, it is recommended to implement strategic tax planning, seek professional assistance, and coordinate with financial goals. Couples can create money and succeed financially in the long run by carefully planning and making wise decisions.

Chapter Six

Handling Financial Difficulties: Methods for Getting Past Roadblocks

Financial difficulties are an unavoidable aspect of money management and wealth accumulation. When pursuing financial independence, a couple may run into a number of challenges, such as unforeseen costs or fluctuations in income. Effectively navigating these obstacles calls for flexibility, strategic planning, and a proactive mindset. This section gives a thorough rundown of the typical financial difficulties that couples encounter and suggests solutions.

1. Dealing with Unexpected Costs

1.1 Establishing an Emergencies Fund:
- **Value:** An emergency fund serves as a safety net for your finances, protecting you from unforeseen costs like auto repairs, medical bills, and job loss. In times of

financial difficulty, having a sizable emergency fund lessens the need to turn to credit cards or loans.

- Financing Methods: Three to six months' worth of living expenditures should be saved. Start off each month with a little, achievable amount, then progressively raise your contributions. Before making significant investments or financial commitments, give priority to establishing this fund.

1.2 Emergency Preparedness:

- Developing a Plan: Create a backup plan that outlines how to handle unforeseen circumstances such as losing your job, needing large repairs, or experiencing an emergency. Incorporate actions like cutting back on discretionary spending, getting insurance, and using neighbourhood resources.

- Insurance Coverage: Make sure you have enough insurance, including disability, house, car, and health insurance. A suitable policy reduces financial risks and guards against large out-of-pocket costs.

2. Handling Variations in Income

2.1 Diversifying Income Streams:

- **Side Hustles and Gig Work:** Look into side gigs, side companies, and other sources of income. Having multiple sources of income lessens the dependence on a single pay cheque and offers stability in the face of market swings.

- **Return on Investment:** Take into account making investments in stocks that provide dividends, real estate, or other assets that generate revenue. Investing in a diversified portfolio can ease financial burden and generate additional income.

2.2 Variability-Based Budgeting:

- **Adaptable Budgeting:** Make a budget that takes fluctuating revenue into account. Set aside money for necessities, give savings top priority, and modify discretionary spending in accordance with your income level right now. Track your income and spending by using apps and tools for budgeting.

- **Managing Cash Flow:** Regularly check cash flow and make any necessary adjustments. Include a cushion in your budget to cover sporadic income and prevent splurging when your income is higher.

3. Taking Care of Debt

3.1 Creating a Plan for Paying Off Debt:
- **Avalanche vs. Snowball Debt:** Select a debt payback plan that complements your financial objectives. While the debt avalanche approach gives priority to high-interest debts in order to reduce total interest payments, the debt snowball method starts with the smallest obligations and works its way up.

- **Debt Consolidation:** Take into account combining several high-interest loans into one with a reduced interest rate. Consolidating debt can lower total interest costs and streamline payments.

3.2 Avoiding New Debt:

- **Smart Borrowing:** Refrain from taking on new debt for luxuries or non-essential goods. Pay off credit card debt in full each month, use credit cards sensibly, and refrain from accruing high-interest debt.

- **Credit Building:** Prioritise establishing and preserving a good credit score by controlling debt levels, using credit responsibly, and making on-time payments. A high credit score can lower borrowing prices and enhance lending terms.

4. Handling Unexpected Debt

4.1 Open Communication:
- **Talking About Finances:** Talk about money issues with your partner on a regular basis to make sure you both understand one other and have similar objectives. Address worries, establish guidelines, and collaborate to discover answers to monetary problems.

- **Looking for Expert Assistance:** If financial stress becomes too much for you to handle, think about speaking with a financial expert or counsellor. Experts can offer advice on investing techniques, debt management, and budgeting.

4.2 Stress Management Techniques:

- **Healthy Habits:** Make use of methods like exercise, mindfulness, and meditation to reduce stress. Sustaining one's physical and mental health can help one make better decisions and be more resilient when faced with financial difficulties.

- **Achieving Practical Objectives:** Set attainable spending targets and acknowledge accomplishments. Stress can be decreased and a sense of success can be gained by breaking down bigger tasks into smaller, more achievable steps.

5. Retirement Planning

5.1 Retirement Savings:

- **Maximising Contributions:** Fund retirement accounts, such as Roth IRAs, 401(k)s, or IRAs, by contributing. To optimise retirement savings, make use of tax breaks and employer-matched contributions.

- Asset Allocation Techniques: Create a diversified investing plan that fits your retirement objectives and risk tolerance. To achieve continuous growth, take into account asset allocation, consistent contributions, and recurring reviews.

5.2 Planning for Retirement:
- Determining Requirements: Calculate your future retirement requirements using your chosen lifestyle, life expectancy, and estimated expenses. To determine whether your existing savings and assets are enough, use retirement calculators and other financial planning tools.

- Modifying Plans: Review retirement plans frequently and make any adjustments. To stay on track for a safe retirement, take into account variables like changes in income, market conditions, and personal objectives.

6. Juggling Your Financial Needs

6.1 Prioritisation:

- **Setting Objectives:** Clearly state your short- and long-term financial objectives, such as building an emergency fund, paying for school, or saving for a house. Sort your goals according to timeliness and importance.

- **Resource Allocation:** Distribute funds according to your priorities. Strike a balance between investing, saving, and spending to create a comprehensive financial strategy that takes care of both short-term and long-term goals.

6.2 Modifying Way of Life:

- **Calculating Trade-Offs:** Be ready to modify your way of life in order to reach your financial objectives. This can entail cutting back on frivolous spending, postponing large purchases, or looking for more affordable options.

- **Assessing Needs against Wants:** Analyse spending patterns on a regular basis to distinguish between necessities and wants. To stay within budget, prioritise meeting basic necessities and cut back on non-essential spending.

7. Tax-related Aspects

7.1 Strategies for Tax Efficiency:
- **Accounts with Tax Advantages:** To optimise tax advantages and lower taxable income, make use of tax-advantaged accounts like 401(k)s, IRAs, and HSAs. Utilise deductions and contributions to reduce your tax obligation.

- **Financial Planning:** To maximise credits, investment techniques, and deductions, engage in proactive tax planning. To create a financially sound plan that minimises taxes, speak with a tax expert.

7.2 Record Keeping:
- **Maintaining Records:** For taxation purposes, maintain correct records of your earnings, outlays, and financial transactions. Accurate tax filings are ensured and

prospective credits or deductions are made easier with proper documentation.

- **Assembling Records:** To track and manage financial documents, use financial software or digital tools. Review and update data on a regular basis to ensure compliance and make tax preparation easier.

A combination of proactive management, flexibility, and strategic planning is needed to overcome financial obstacles. Couples can overcome challenges and establish a solid financial foundation by handling unforeseen expenses, controlling income changes, managing debt, reducing financial stress, and making retirement plans. Financial resilience is further enhanced by establishing priorities, making lifestyle adjustments, and taking tax consequences into account. Couples can effectively manage financial problems and accomplish their financial goals together with the help of effective techniques and continuous communication.

➢ Resolving Conflicts: Handling Money Issues in a Partnership

Couples striving for financial independence frequently encounter money arguments. Relationships and financial well-being may suffer as a result of disagreements over spending patterns, priorities for saving, and financial objectives. To effectively tackle and settle these conflicts, compromise, empathy, and open communication are necessary. The methods for resolving financial disputes and identifying common ground are covered in this section.

1. Opening Up Lines of Communication

1.1 Establishing a Secure Environment for Conversation:
- **Promoting Honest Communication:** Provide a space where both spouses may freely discuss their financial worries and thoughts without worrying about criticism or

reprisals. Instead of approaching conversations with an attitude of conflict, adopt a collaborative one.

- **Frequent Updates on Finances:** Call frequent meetings to talk over financial issues such as goal advancement, expenditures, and budgeting. Regular check-ins help avoid misunderstandings and guarantee that both parties are still focused on the same financial goals.

1.2 Listening While Active:

- **Listening without Distracting:** By allowing your spouse to speak uninterrupted, you can engage in active listening. Prior to answering or making suggestions, concentrate on learning about their viewpoint and issues.

- **Confirming Emotions:** Even if you disagree, respect and acknowledge each other's emotions and points of view. During conversations, empathetic and understanding behaviour helps to foster trust and ease tension.

2. Determining the Sources of Conflicts

2.1 Examining Root Causes:

- **Investigating Motives:** Consider the fundamental causes of financial conflicts, such as conflicting moral principles, financial strain, or traumatic events. By addressing the underlying causes instead of just the symptoms, it is possible to treat the main problems.

- **Recognising Triggers:** Identify the particular triggers, such as major purchases, unforeseen expenses, or disparities in spending patterns, that result in financial problems. By recognising these triggers, conflicts can be avoided in the future and proactive management can be implemented.

2.2 Addressing Financial Goals and Values:

- **Aligning Values:** Talk about and come to an agreement on priorities and financial values. Comprehending the financial objectives and driving forces of each partner facilitates the development of a common vision and lessens problems arising from divergent values.

- **Assigning Shared Objectives:** Decide on shared financial objectives that the two of you can work towards. A feeling of direction and purpose that comes from having shared goals makes it simpler to resolve conflicts and maintain focus on long-term goals.

3. Formulating Powerful Techniques for Resolving Conflict

3.1 Negotiation and Compromise:

- **Finding Middle Ground:** Collaborate to identify a compromise that meets the requirements and preferences of both parties. To find a solution that works for everyone, think about settling on conditions or making changes to your saving and spending plans.

- **Flexibility:** Be prepared to modify financial objectives and plans as necessary. Being flexible makes it possible to respect each partner's choices and resolve disagreements amicably.

3.2 Determining Budgetary Boundaries:

- **Determining Caps:** Decide on the financial parameters and restrictions for investments, savings, and discretionary expenditures. Having defined boundaries aids in avoiding problems arising from excessive spending or divergent financial priorities.

- **Establishing Guidelines for Major Buyings:** Establish a procedure for major financial decisions, such as establishing shared approval thresholds or mandating a conversation prior to major purchases. This guarantees a voice for each spouse in significant financial choices.

4. Making Use of Expert Help

4.1 Seeking Guidance on Finances:
- **Assisting an Expert:** If arguments don't go away or get out of control, think about getting help from a therapist or financial counsellor. Professionals are able to mediate disputes, enhance communication, and offer unbiased advice.

- **Counseling's Benefits:** Couples who receive financial counselling can enhance their communication abilities, create efficient money management plans, and deal with underlying problems that cause financial arguments.

4.2 Educational Materials:

- **Money Management:** Make an investment in money management materials, such books, seminars, or online courses. Developing a greater comprehension of financial ideas and tactics might help decision-makers make better choices and handle money management issues less frequently.

- **Cooperative Education:** As a group, engage in financial education activities to develop common knowledge and abilities. Collaborating while learning improves teamwork and your capacity to handle financial difficulties.

5. Putting Integrated Financial Planning Into Practice

5.1 Joint Spending:

- Making a Shared Budget: Create a shared budget that accounts for the income, expenses, and financial objectives of both spouses. Transparency is offered by a shared budget, which also ensures that partners are in agreement about how much to spend and save.

- Monitoring Development: Review and update the joint budget on a regular basis to monitor progress and make necessary adjustments. Together, you can monitor your budget to ensure responsibility and resolve any anomalies or problems that may occur.

5.2 Together Setting Financial Goals:

- Goal Setting: Identify and rank financial objectives that complement each partner's values and aspirations. Establishing common objectives facilitates collaboration in the pursuit of financial milestones by offering guidance and inspiration.

- Recognising Success: As a pair, commemorate financial milestones and accomplishments.

Acknowledging and praising accomplishments encourage constructive behaviour and improve the working relationship.

6. Keeping Up a Good Connection

6.1 Promoting Respect for One Another:
- **Accepting Differences:** Be mindful of one another's financial preferences and opinions, even if they diverge from your own. A respectful and well-functioning relationship is facilitated by acknowledging and appreciating each partner's viewpoint.

- **Avoiding Blame:** Put more effort into coming up with fixes than placing blame. Assigning blame to one spouse for financial issues breeds resentment and impedes growth. Adopt a problem-solving approach while dealing with conflicts.

6.2 Establishing Trust and Support:
- **Helping One Another:** Offer consolation and inspiration while facing financial difficulties.

Establishing mutual trust and exhibiting a dedication to each other's financial well fortifies the alliance and improves cooperation.

- **Sustaining Equilibrium:** Counterbalance monetary conversations with gratifying exchanges of ideas and experiences. Maintaining overall relationship pleasure involves making sure that money-related concerns don't take precedence over other parts of the partnership.

Effectively resolving financial conflicts calls for cooperation, empathy, and open communication. Couples can overcome financial obstacles and improve their relationship by creating a safe environment for communication, figuring out the underlying reasons for problems, and coming up with creative ways to resolve conflicts. Long-term financial independence and effective money management are further enhanced by hiring a professional adviser, carrying out joint financial planning, and preserving a positive working relationship. Couples can resolve financial disagreements and accomplish their shared financial objectives by showing respect and encouragement for one another.

➢ Planning for Major Life Events: Ensuring Success and Financial Stability

Achieving financial independence as a marriage requires careful planning for significant life events. Big life decisions like buying a house, having children, or retiring can have a big impact on finances. Efficient preparation for these occasions reduces stress, helps maintain financial security, and empowers couples to make wise choices. This section looks at ways to get ready for big life events, including making a detailed plan, defining financial objectives, and dealing with obstacles.

1. Recognising Significant Life Events

1.1 Typical Significant Life Events:

- **Home Purchasing:** Significant financial obligations are involved in buying a property, including down payments, mortgage payments, and continuing upkeep expenses. Creating a budget, obtaining financing, and evaluating your financial preparedness are all necessary steps in the house buying process.

- **Family Formation:** There are additional costs associated with starting a family, such as prenatal care, childbirth, and daycare. Financial stability depends on setting aside money for these fees and making plans for future educational needs.

- **Security:** Saving and investing are part of retirement planning in order to guarantee a safe and enjoyable retirement. It necessitates projecting future costs, figuring out how much savings are needed, and selecting sensible investment plans.

1.2 Evaluating the Financial Effect:
- **Assessing the Expenses:** Evaluate each significant life event's financial impact by projecting related expenses

and determining how well they align with your overall financial strategy. Take into account both one-time costs and continuing financial obligations.

- **Modifying Budgetary Objectives:** Modify your priorities and financial objectives to account for significant life events. This could entail changing your budget, reallocating resources, or modifying your investment and savings plans.

2. Formulating an All-encompassing Scheme

2.1 Defining Objectives:
- **Setting Financial Goals:** Make sure your financial goals are clear for every significant life event. Establish targets for the down payment amount, the length of the mortgage, and the cost of house maintenance, for instance, if you're buying a property.

- **Determining Schedules:** Establish reasonable deadlines for reaching your financial objectives. Think about how long it will take to save for a down payment, plan for the costs of childbirth, or accumulate retirement savings.

2.2 Setting Up a Budget and Saving:
- **Creating a Budget:** Make a thorough budget that accounts for projected expenses related to all significant life events. Include these expenses in your monthly budget and monitor your progress towards setting aside the required amount of money.

- **Creating a Plan for Savings:** Create a savings strategy that complements your financial objectives. Think about creating specialised savings accounts for particular life events, such a fund for a child's education or a home purchase.

2.3 Prudent Investing:
- **Selecting Investment Approaches:** Make investment decisions based on timetables and financial objectives. Think about a diverse investment portfolio that strikes a balance between risk and return for long-term objectives like retirement.

- **Continually Examining Investments:** To make sure your investment portfolio stays in line with your objectives and risk tolerance, examine and alter it on a regular basis. To maximise your investing strategy, think about collaborating with a financial advisor.

3. Dealing with Possible Difficulties

3.1 Managing Unexpected Expenses:

- **Building an Emergency Fund:** Set aside money for unforeseen costs that might come up during significant life events. Make sure you have enough money saved up for living expenses for at least three or six months.

- **Emergency Preparedness:** Create backup plans in case you face financial difficulties due to things like job loss or unforeseen medical bills. To reduce risks, think about insurance alternatives like property, health, and disability insurance.

3.2 Adapting to Life Transitions:

- **Handling Financial Changes:** Significant lifestyle changes are frequently the result of major life events. If your income, expenses, or financial responsibilities change, be ready to make adjustments to your financial plans and budget.

- **Handling Uncertainty and Stress:** Significant life events can cause anxiety and uncertainty. Utilise stress-reduction strategies, such as communication and mindfulness, to preserve your mental and financial health.

4. Working together to plan finances

4.1 Collaborating as a Group:
- **Shared Decision-Making:** As a pair, decide on financial matters while taking each other's preferences and points of view into account. Making decisions together improves understanding between spouses and fortifies your financial relationship.

- **Consistent Communication:** Keep lines of communication open regarding your financial goals, achievements, and obstacles. Review your financial strategy frequently and make any necessary revisions.

4.2 Seeking Professional guidance:
- **Consulting Financial Experts:** To assist you manage difficult financial decisions and maximise your financial strategy, think about getting guidance from financial professionals, such as financial advisers, tax planners, or estate planners.

- **Utilising Resources:** To improve your knowledge of financial planning and help you make wise decisions, make use of resources including financial planning tools, workshops, and instructional materials.

5. Retirement Planning

5.1 Calculating Expenses for Retirement:
- **Calculate Expenses:** Compute your anticipated future living, medical, and lifestyle expenditures for retirement.

When making retirement plans, take into account variables like inflation and shifting healthcare requirements.

- Calculating the Need for Savings: Determine how much money you'll need to save for retirement. To grow your retirement fund, think about retirement savings accounts like 401(k)s, IRAs, and other investment vehicles.

5.2 Creating a Plan for Retirement:

- Choosing Retirement Accounts: Make sure your retirement accounts reflect your tax choices and goals. Think about individual retirement accounts (IRAs), employer-sponsored plans, and other investing possibilities.

- Developing a Plan for Withdrawal: Create a strategy for taking out money when you retire. Take into account things like the sustainability of your retirement assets, tax ramifications, and required minimum distributions (RMDs).

6. Financial Planning for the Long Term

6.1 Establishing Extended Objectives:

- **Specifying Future Goals:** Determine long-term financial objectives, such as providing for a legacy, accumulating money, or financing school. Plan these objectives in accordance with your significant life events to guarantee a well-coordinated financial plan.

- **Travelling Forward:** Review and modify your long-term financial strategy on a regular basis to take goals, circumstances, and financial markets into consideration. To stay on course, keep an eye on your development and make any required corrections.

6.2 Preserving Adaptability:

- **Adjusting to Shifts:** Be ready to modify your financial plan to account for shifts in your circumstances, including changes in your family, work, or health. Maintaining flexibility helps to keep your plan current and functional.

- **Continuous Learning:** Keep up with the latest tactics, trends, and best practices in finance. You can make wise judgements and adjust to changing financial environments with the support of ongoing education.

Achieving financial independence as a marriage requires careful planning for significant life events. Couples can handle significant life transitions with confidence and financial stability by identifying important events, developing a thorough plan, addressing potential obstacles, and working well together. Couples may make sure they are ready for the financial ramifications of big life changes and collaborate to reach their long-term financial objectives by carefully planning their budget, saving, and investing.

➤ Seeking Professional Advice

Getting expert counsel is essential to becoming financially independent as a marriage. Financial specialists can offer insightful advice, practical tactics, and direction to improve your financial planning and more successfully assist you reach your objectives. This section looks at the value of speaking with financial experts, the kinds of specialists you should talk to, and how to take full use of their advice.

1. The Significance of Expert Guidance

1.1 Knowledge and Background:
When negotiating complex financial decisions, the depth of knowledge and experience that financial professionals bring can be extremely helpful. They give you knowledgeable advice that is specific to your circumstances by staying up to date on the most recent developments in tax legislation, investment techniques, and financial trends.

1.2 An Objective Viewpoint:
An unbiased assessment of your financial status is offered by a financial counsellor. They can assist you in addressing possible hazards, identifying blind spots, and

making data-driven decisions as opposed to gut feelings. When handling delicate financial concerns together, this objectivity can be quite helpful.

1.3 Tailored Approaches:

Experts in finance provide tailored approaches based on your individual objectives, risk appetite, and financial situation. They can create plans that meet your needs and assist you in reaching your goals, whether you're investing for the future, managing debt, or planning for retirement.

2. Categories of Financial Experts

2.1 Role of Financial Advisors: Comprehensive financial planning services, such as risk management, retirement planning, and investment management, are offered by financial advisors. Together, you and they create a financial strategy that fits your objectives and risk tolerance.

- **Types:** Financial advisors can work as commission-based advisors, fee-only advisors, or a combination of the two. It's critical to comprehend their price schedule and how it could affect their advice.

2.2 Tax Consultants:

- **Position:** Tax planning and optimisation are areas of expertise for tax consultants. They assure tax law compliance, help you maximise credits and deductions, and help you grasp the tax ramifications. Tax consultants can also help with large financial event planning and tax-efficient investing options.

- **Types:** Tax attorneys, enrolled agents, and certified public accountants (CPAs) are examples of tax counsellors. Select a tax counsel who is knowledgeable about your unique tax circumstances and requirements.

2.3. The role of Estate Planners: The main goal of estate planners is to assist you in making arrangements for the transfer of your assets upon death. They offer assistance with creating trusts, writing wills, and taking estate tax issues into account. Estate planning can assist reduce your heirs' tax obligations and guarantees that your assets are dispersed in accordance with your desires.

- **Types:** Estate planners might be registered estate planning specialists, financial planners with estate planning experience, or lawyers with specialised estate planning training.

2.4 Advisors for Investments:

- **Post:** Creating investment plans and managing investment portfolios are the areas of expertise for investment advisors. They assist you in selecting assets that are suitable for your objectives, level of risk tolerance, and time horizon. Advisors on investments may also offer advice on portfolio diversification and asset allocation.

- **Types:** Investment advisers can be employed by independent advisors, financial institutions, or investment firms. Seek out consultants that possess the necessary credentials, such as Certified Financial Planner (CFP) or Chartered Financial Analyst (CFA).

3. Selecting the Appropriate Expert

3.1 Evaluating Your Requirements:
- **Establish Your Objectives:** Determine your needs and financial objectives before consulting a specialist. Knowing your goals will help you select the best expert, whether you're investing, managing debt, or planning for retirement.

- **Assess Expertise:** Seek out experts in the fields where you require direction. For instance, look for a financial advisor with experience in retirement plans if you need assistance with retirement planning.

3.2 Experts in Research:
- **Verify Credentials:** Check the references and credentials of possible advisors. Seek out credentials that attest to a high degree of competence and adherence to professional norms, such as CFP, CFA, or CPA.

- Examine the Citations and Reviews: To evaluate the advisor's standing and efficacy, look up reviews online and ask for recommendations from previous customers. Individual referrals from reliable sources may also be beneficial.

3.3 Understanding Compensation and Fees:

- Fee arrangements: Recognise the potential advisors' fee arrangements. While some advisors take a fixed fee, others might base their fees on the assets they manage or get commissions from the sale of their products. Select a cost schedule that both satisfies your needs and guarantees openness.

- Arbitration of Interest: Recognise any possible conflicts of interest. Make sure the advisor is acting in your best interest and isn't being swayed by commissions or other rewards.

4. Utilising Expert Guidance to the Fullest

4.1 Clearly Defined Expectations:

- **Establish Goals:** Tell the counsellor exactly what you hope to achieve financially. This guarantees that you are both on the same page and helps them customise their advice to your particular needs.

- **Create a Communication Channel:** Establish guidelines for the frequency and style of communication. You may stay updated about the status and plan of your finances with regular updates and conversations.

4.2 Examining and Modifying:

- **Conducting Regular Reviews:** Arrange for frequent evaluations with your advisor to evaluate the advancement of your financial strategy. Examine goal attainment, budget modifications, and investment performance to make sure your strategy stays in line with your goals.

- **Modifying Techniques:** Be willing to modify your plans in response to fresh facts or evolving conditions. Your financial strategy should be adaptable enough to take into account shifting objectives, market conditions, and changes in your life.

4.3 Self-Education:
- Learning Occasions: Make use of the materials, classes, and seminars that your adviser offers as educational opportunities. Knowing the fundamentals of finance enables you to participate in the planning process more skilfully and to make well-informed judgements.

- Proposing Queries: Never be afraid to clarify anything you don't understand about finances by asking questions. A competent advisor will make the effort to clarify difficult ideas and make sure you comprehend their suggestions.

5. Including Expert Guidance in Your Financial Strategy

5.1 Organising alongside Other Experts:
- Teamwork Method: To make sure that every part of your financial strategy is integrated, collaborate with

other experts like estate planners or tax counsellors. Professional cooperation facilitates the development of a comprehensive plan that takes care of all your financial requirements.

5.2 Putting Suggestions into Practice:
- **Action Plan:** Create a plan of action based on the advisor's suggestions. Putting their recommendations into practice entails performing certain actions, such as modifying your financial portfolio, making a budget, or opening retirement accounts.

5.3 Tracking Development:
- **Monitoring Outcomes:** When you follow professional guidance, keep an eye on the outcomes and evaluate how they affect your financial objectives. To stay on course, check your progress frequently and make necessary adjustments.

One of the most important steps towards achieving financial independence as a couple is consulting a specialist. Experts in finance can provide insightful analysis, tailored plans, and impartial viewpoints to improve your financial planning and decision-making. You can manage difficult financial decisions, accomplish your objectives, and create a safe financial future together by selecting the proper experts, establishing clear expectations, and incorporating their guidance into your financial plan. Expert advice is essential to securing your financial success, whether you're investing for the future, managing debt, or planning for retirement.

Chapter Seven

Maintaining Financial Harmony: Methods for Partnerships

Sustaining financial balance is essential to any relationship's success. Although managing finances can sometimes lead to stress and conflict, couples can manage their money in a way that improves rather than weakens their relationship with the correct techniques and honest communication. Effective strategies for preserving financial harmony are examined in this part, with a focus on proactive management, agreed goals, and communication.

1. Honest Communication

1.1 Creating a Secure Environment:
Establishing a safe atmosphere where both parties feel comfortable talking about money is necessary for open discussion about finances. Steer clear of judgement and

blame. Prioritise mutual understanding and problem-solving while having financial conversations. It can be beneficial to schedule regular time for money talks to keep both spouses informed and engaged.

1.2 Establishing Protocols for Communication:
Creating rules for talking about money might help avoid misunderstandings and confrontations. Establish a polite tone, refrain from interjecting, and make sure that each partner gets an equal chance to voice their opinions. Communication can be better managed by scheduling regular meetings for financial topics, such as yearly financial planning sessions or weekly budget reviews.

1.3 Dealing with Emotional Elements:
Emotional topics like tension, worry, or conflicting values are frequently brought up in conversations about money. Openly acknowledge and deal with these feelings. Comprehending one another's financial anxieties, goals, and principles helps foster empathy and minimise discord. If financial stress becomes too much

for you to handle, think about getting help from a financial therapist or counsellor.

2. Determining Mutual Financial Objectives

2.1 Creating Shared Goals:
Achieving financial harmony requires setting common financial goals. Talk about your long- and short-term objectives, like house ownership, retirement savings, and vacation preparation. By ensuring that both partners are working towards the same goals, aligning your financial goals promotes cooperation and teamwork.

2.2 Setting Goal Priorities:
After you've determined your objectives, rank them according to significance and deadlines. Ascertain which objectives are short-term and long-term. Setting priorities guarantees that resources are allocated efficiently and keeps both spouses concentrated on completing the most crucial tasks first.

2.3 Examining and Modifying Objectives:

Review and modify your financial goals on a regular basis. Events in life, including moving jobs, growing a family, or changes in the economy, might affect your priorities and aspirations. Regular evaluations make sure your objectives are still relevant and attainable and provide you the opportunity to make changes in response to evolving conditions.

3. Creating a Collaborative Budget

3.1 Developing a Joint Budget:
The foundation of financial peace is a shared budget. List all of your sources of income and spending first. Sort spending into fixed (such as utilities and a mortgage) and variable (such as grocery and entertainment) categories. Divide the money among the categories according to your priorities and financial objectives.

3.2 Keeping Account of and Handling Bills:
To efficiently manage your budget and keep track of your spending, use applications or tools for budgeting.

Keeping an eye on your expenditures might help you spot areas where you might be overspending or where you can cut back. Reviewing your budget jointly on a regular basis encourages accountability and keeps both parties in agreement.

3.3 Making Budget Adjustments:
Your budget may need to be adjusted due to unforeseen costs or changes in your life. Be adaptable and prepared to make necessary revisions to your budget. Decide how to handle any changes by having an open discussion about them. For instance, you might need to modify your budget to account for a partner's shift in income if they lose their job.

4. Sharing Accountable Duties

4.1 Role Assignment:
To prevent misunderstandings and guarantee that both partners participate in money management, clearly outline financial duties. Bill payment may fall within one partner's purview while savings or investments are

managed by the other. Assign duties according to the preferences and strengths of each couple.

4.2 Division of Duties:
Major financial choices and planning should involve both partners, even if one takes on additional financial responsibilities. Inform each other on a regular basis about financial decisions and issues. Assuring that all parties are informed and involved is facilitated by the sharing of responsibilities.

4.3 Dealing with Inequalities:
Talk frankly about any inequities in financial duties or feelings of overwhelm experienced by one partner. To guarantee that both partners are equally active and that nobody feels overburdened, reassess and shift tasks as necessary.

5. Resolving Conflicts Regarding Money

5.1 Determining the Fundamental Cause:

Determine the underlying reason of disputes when they occur. Is there a difference in priorities, values, or spending patterns? Finding common ground and resolving the conflict more skilfully can be achieved by comprehending the underlying problem.

5.2 Making Compromises and Solving Them:
Collaborate to identify solutions that satisfy the requirements and preferences of each partner. Finding a middle ground on spending patterns, changing financial goals, or modifying budgets are some examples of compromise. When confronted with conflicts, adopt a problem-solving attitude and a cooperative spirit.

5.3 Looking for a Mediator:
If arguments continue or become really difficult, think about getting a financial counsellor or therapist to mediate the conflict. A third party that is impartial can help to organise talks, find answers, and offer dispute resolution techniques.

6. Establishing Transparency and Trust

6.1 Being Truthful Regarding Money:

Being truthful is essential to preserving financial balance. Be open and honest about your earnings, outlays, debts, and financial objectives. Withholding financial information or making covert purchases can erode confidence and lead to disputes. Transparently communicate financial data and address any worries or problems.

6.2 Honouring Financial Achievements:

Together, commemorate financial accomplishments and milestones. Acknowledge and celebrate any success made towards your objectives, whether it's debt repayment, saving a certain amount of money, or hitting a financial milestone. Honouring accomplishments fortifies your relationship and encourages constructive behaviour.

6.3 Establishing Structural Stability:

By managing debt, setting up an emergency fund, and making plans for future expenses, you may increase your financial resilience. A solid financial base reduces anxiety and gives one a sense of stability. Collaborate to develop and preserve your financial resilience so that you are equipped to deal with obstacles and unforeseen circumstances.

7. Developing and Strengthening One Another

7.1 Information Exchange About Finances:

Inform one another about ideas, tactics, and resources related to money. By exchanging information, partners improve their financial literacy and are able to make more educated decisions. Take online courses, read books, or attend workshops to deepen your grasp of personal finance.

7.2 Fostering Mutual Development:

Encourage one another to reach their individual financial objectives, such as raising savings, decreasing debt, or enhancing credit scores. Encourage one another to seek out financial development and education. Mutual support promotes confidence-building and a team-based approach to money management.

7.3 Promoting Responsibility:

Be responsible for each other's financial actions and decisions. Review goals' progress on a regular basis, talk about obstacles, and acknowledge accomplishments. Accountability makes it more likely that both partners will stick to their budget and keep pursuing their goals.

It takes proactive management, open communication, and agreed goals to maintain financial harmony in a relationship. Couples may create a solid financial foundation that supports their objectives and relationship by setting up a safe space for discussions, making joint budgets, assigning duties, and resolving conflicts. Financial harmony is further enhanced by fostering mutual trust, educating one another, and commemorating achievements. Couples can effectively manage their financial journey and attain financial independence jointly if they adopt a cooperative mindset and make a commitment to understanding one another.

➢ Promoting Open Communication: The Foundation of Stability in Money

Any successful relationship must have effective communication, and when it comes to money, it's even more important for keeping things harmonious and accomplishing common objectives. Encouraging candid dialogue about finances aids in navigating financial choices, settling disputes, and laying a strong basis for the future for a relationship. The methods for encouraging honest and beneficial financial conversations are covered in this section.

1. Establishing a Secure Environment

1.1 Building Confidence:
Trust is the foundation of a secure environment for financial conversations. It should be acceptable for both partners to discuss their ideas, worries, and financial situation without fear of rebuke or condemnation. Being truthful, sympathetic, and impartial in talks is essential to

building trust. Couples are able to have an open discussion without feeling attacked or defensive when they are in a supportive atmosphere.

1.2 Selecting the Appropriate Time:
Choose the right moments to have financial conversations. When things are difficult or emotionally heated, don't discuss money matters. Instead, pick periods that are neutral and quiet for both spouses. Another way to make sure that talks are conducted consistently and without the strain of pressing issues is to schedule frequent finance sessions.

1.3 Creating a Happy Atmosphere:
Be cooperative and positive when having financial conversations. Instead of placing blame or criticism on others, choose language that highlights cooperation and common aims. "Let's work on this together" and "How can we solve this issue?" are examples of phrases that foster respect and collaboration.

2. Paying Attention

2.1 Being Present in Whole:

Being totally present during talks is a necessary part of active listening. Give your partner your whole attention, refrain from interjecting, and show that you respect their viewpoint. In addition to demonstrating respect, this ensures that each partner feels heard and understood.

2.2 Contemplating and Expliciting:

Consider what your colleague has stated by summarising or paraphrasing their main points. By posing open-ended enquiries, you can clear up any confusion or misunderstandings. For instance, "Can you explain more about what you mean?" Alternatively "I want to make sure I understand your concerns correctly."

2.3 Acknowledging Emotions:

Respect and validate one another's thoughts and emotions. Even if you don't entirely agree, acknowledging and valuing your partner's feelings improves empathy and fortifies your relationship. Expressions of support and empathy such as "I can see why you feel that way" or "I understand that this is important to you" are helpful.

3. Collaborating to Set Financial Objectives

3.1 Determining Common Objectives:
Establishing mutual financial objectives promotes cooperation and helps partners' priorities line up. Talk about your short- and long-term objectives, such as debt management, retirement planning, and house savings. Establishing shared goals guarantees that all parties are aiming for the same financial results.

3.2 Setting Goal Priorities:
After you've determined what your goals are, order them according to priority and deadline. Decide which objectives must be met right now and which can wait. Setting priorities guarantees that resources are allocated efficiently and keeps both partners concentrated on completing the most important tasks first.

3.3 Reviewing Objectives Frequently:

Make sure your financial goals are still relevant and attainable by reviewing and evaluating them on a regular basis. Your goals and priorities may alter as a result of life events like changing careers, expanding families, or adverse economic times. Regular evaluations keep both parties informed and in sync by assisting with necessary objective and strategy adjustments.

4. Resolving Conflicts Regarding Money

4.1 Finding the Primary Cause:
Determine the root cause of disputes as soon as they occur. Does this have to do with priorities, finances, or values? Finding a common ground and addressing the problem more skilfully are made possible by knowing the root reason.

4.2 Making concessions and resolving issues:
Collaborate to identify solutions that satisfy the requirements and preferences of each partner. Finding a middle ground on spending habits, modifying financial goals, or tweaking budgets are some examples of

compromise. When confronted with conflicts, adopt a problem-solving attitude and a cooperative spirit.

4.3 Looking for a Mediator:

If arguments continue or become really difficult, think about getting a financial counsellor or therapist to mediate the conflict. A third party that is impartial can help to organise talks, find answers, and offer dispute resolution techniques. One useful method for resolving difficult or pervasive problems is mediation.

5. Sincerity and Openness

5.1 Disclosure of Financial Data:

To preserve confidence and maintain financial harmony, transparency is essential. Provide pertinent financial data, such as earnings, outlays, debts, and savings. Withholding financial information or making covert purchases can erode confidence and lead to disputes. Talk honestly about your finances and any changes that might affect your relationship.

5.2 Talking About Financial Difficulties:

Openly and truthfully discuss any financial difficulties or worries you may have. Whether it's handling debt, handling unforeseen costs, or adjusting to salary fluctuations, talking about these problems with your partner can help you discover answers and make sure you both understand the circumstances.

5.3 Establishing Credibility:

Reliability and integrity in financial concerns must be continuously demonstrated in order to establish and preserve trust. Keep your word, be truthful while making financial decisions, and cooperate with others to overcome obstacles. A solid financial relationship is built on trust.

6. Teaching and Motivating One Another

6.1 Information Exchange About Finances:

Inform one another about ideas, tactics, and resources related to money. Exchange materials to improve your knowledge of personal finance, such as financial planning tools, books, and articles. Learning jointly fosters confidence in financial management and enables both spouses to make well-informed decisions.

6.2 Fostering Mutual Development:

Encourage one another's personal financial development. Set personal objectives, support one another's financial education endeavours, and hone your financial literacy. Mutual support promotes confidence-building and a team-based approach to money management.

6.3 Promoting Responsibility:

Be responsible for each other's financial actions and decisions. Review goals' progress on a regular basis, talk about obstacles, and acknowledge accomplishments. Accountability guarantees that each partner stays dedicated to their financial plan and keeps pursuing their goals.

7. Honouring Financial Achievements

7.1 Acknowledging Success:

Together, commemorate financial accomplishments and milestones. Whether it's debt repayment, savings, or money management, recognising and applauding accomplishments improves your relationship and encourages positive behaviour.

7.2 Honouring Development:
Think about rewarding yourself when you hit financial benchmarks. Simple rewards like a special dinner, a modest purchase, or an excursion can be given out. Honouring accomplishments keeps one's motivation high and promotes a good outlook on money management.

7.3 Examining Achievement:
Think back on your experience and the strides you've made in achieving your financial objectives. Talk about the things that went well, the difficulties you encountered, and how you handled them. Thinking back on your accomplishments gives you insights for future financial planning and serves to promote positive behaviours.

Encouraging candid conversations about money is crucial to keeping the peace and becoming financially successful as a partnership. Couples can navigate their financial path together by establishing a safe environment for discussions, actively listening to each other, defining goals, resolving arguments, and developing trust. Financial harmony is further enhanced by recognising accomplishments, encouraging each other's growth, and upholding transparency. Couples can attain their shared goals and create a solid financial foundation by working together and communicating well, which will improve their personal and financial relationships.

➤ Celebrating Financial Milestones

Marking the completion of a savings goal or debt payback is not the only reason to celebrate financial milestones; it's also an opportunity to reward good effort, encourage positive behaviour, and fortify the financial bond between partners. Acknowledging and enjoying successes as a group improves teamwork, motivates employees, and makes the financial path more fulfilling. This section examines the value of commemorating accomplishments, doable celebration ideas, and associated advantages.

1. Acknowledging Success

1.1 Highlighting Achievements:
The first step in identifying financial milestones is to celebrate every accomplishment, no matter how big or small. Every achievement is worthy of praise, whether it's meeting a savings target, paying off a sizable amount of debt, or successfully adhering to a budget for a predetermined amount of time. This acknowledgement strengthens the dedication to achieving financial goals and helps to validate the work performed.

1.2 Progress Reporting:
By keeping a record of your progress, you can keep track of your financial achievements. Make a visual depiction

of your progress, such a milestone board or progress chart, to help you see your development. This can be a useful strategy for maintaining motivation and celebrating successes.

1.3 Achievement in Sharing:
As a team, celebrate your accomplishments and let each other know about them. Talking about and thinking back on your progress as a team strengthens the bond between you and your combined effort. It also enables the couple to celebrate the trip and recognise each other's contributions.

2. Commending Achievement

2.1 Establishing Reward Standards:
Establish criteria for awards that are consistent with your values and financial objectives. Determine in advance what kind of award is acceptable and what milestones call for one. This could be reaching a savings goal, paying off a specific amount of debt, or adhering to a budget for a number of months.

2.2 Selecting Significant Incentives:

Choose rewards that both couples will find fun and meaningful. Rewards can change based on your preferences and financial status. They might be a small item you've been saving for, a weekend excursion, or a nice supper out. The secret is to select prizes that both honour your accomplishments and fit into your overall spending strategy.

2.3 Juggling Pleasure and Budget:

Make sure the incentives you select don't interfere with your financial plan. Celebrate accomplishments in a way that advances rather than undermines your financial objectives. For instance, think of a small incentive that doesn't interfere with your savings strategy if you're saving for a big buy.

3. Examining Achievements

3.1 Examining Accomplishments:

Give yourself some time to go over and consider your achievements. Talk about the things that went well, the tactics you used, and the obstacles you overcome. Thinking back on accomplishments gives significant insights for future financial planning and serves to promote excellent behaviours.

3.2 Assessing Advancement:
Assess the strides you've made in achieving your financial objectives. Evaluate the effects of reaching milestones on your entire financial situation and make any necessary modifications. Make new goals and adjustments to your financial strategies using this reflection.

3.3 Taking A Lesson From The Trip:
Honour the knowledge you have gained from your financial path. Think about the lessons your accomplishments have taught you about goal-setting, collaboration, and your financial habits. Accept these insights to fortify your connection and enhance your financial procedures going forward.

4. Fortifying Your Monetary Connection

4.1 Improving Collaboration:

Collaborating and working as a team is strengthened when milestones are celebrated jointly. Recognise each partner's contribution to reaching the financial objectives and thank them for it. This strengthens the relationship between the two people and inspires them to keep collaborating to achieve their goals.

4.2 Creating a Positive Flow:

Celebrating victories promotes continuing advancement and good energy. Acknowledging successes makes both spouses feel accomplished and encourages them to stick to their budget. It supports the notion that success is the result of perseverance and hard work.

4.3 Enhancing Interaction:

Partner communication is improved when financial accomplishments are celebrated and discussed. It offers a chance to talk about future objectives, express satisfaction, and address any worries. Improved communication fosters a cooperative approach to financial management and aids in the preservation of financial harmony.

5. Including Holidays in Your Daily Activities

5.1 Arrangement Frequent Visits:
Make sure your financial regimen includes frequent check-ins to assess progress and recognise accomplishments. Call meetings on a weekly or quarterly basis to review progress, establish new objectives, and recognise accomplishments. Frequent check-ins guarantee that both spouses are actively participating in the financial journey and help keep things focused.

5.2 Establishing Customs:
Create customs for marking anniversaries that are significant to both couples. This could be an annual trip to celebrate advancement, an elegant dinner, or an assessment of financial results. Establishing traditions improves the financial journey's enjoyment and serves to promote beneficial behaviours.

5.3 Involvement with Close Those:

When you reach financial milestones, think about sharing them with loved ones who encourage you on your path. Celebrating with those you love can boost your motivation and give you a greater sense of accomplishment. It also enables you to get support and affirmation from people who are close to you.

6. Juggling Celebration with Persistent Work

6.1 Steer Clear of Complacency:

As vital as it is to recognise accomplishments, it is just as critical to stay away from complacency. Instead of viewing accomplishments as a destination, use them as stepping stones for future development. Remain committed to your long-term financial goals and keep pushing for new accomplishments.

6.2 Creating New Objectives:

To maintain momentum after celebrating a milestone, create new objectives. Specify your future goals and devise a strategy to accomplish them. Establishing fresh objectives guarantees that you stay committed to the financial path and keep moving forward.

6.3 Accepting the Adventure:

Accept the financial journey as an ongoing process of development and progress. Honour accomplishments, draw lessons from setbacks, and take pleasure in the advancements gained along the route. You and your partner can stay motivated and create a more secure financial future if you approach the road with optimism.

Building and preserving financial harmony as a couple requires celebrating financial accomplishments. A constructive and cooperative financial journey is facilitated by acknowledging accomplishments, praising advancement, thinking back on accomplishments, and fortifying your financial relationship. Remaining successful and motivated can be ensured by including celebrations into your routine, striking a balance between celebration and ongoing effort, and setting new goals. Couples can strengthen positive behaviours, improve teamwork, and reap the benefits of their combined efforts by commemorating milestones together.

➢ Adapting and Evolving: Handling Monetary Shifts Together

The capacity to change and grow is essential on the path to becoming financially independent and accumulating money as a pair. Over time, financial circumstances, objectives, and surroundings may change. To effectively manage these changes, one must be adaptable, resilient, and proactive in their planning. This part looks at how important it is to adjust to changes in your finances, how to update your financial plan over time, and how teamwork and communication may help you get through these changes.

1. Accepting Modification

1.1 Recognising Changes in Finances:

A number of factors, including changes in income, employment status, family dynamics, or general economic situations, can lead to changes in one's finances. To effectively adapt, one must first acknowledge these changes. Accept change as a necessary component of both life and financial planning, and approach it with optimism.

1.2 Evaluating Effect:

Analyse the effects of changes on your goals and financial status. For example, losing your work could have an impact on your income and spending plan, and adding a new family member could necessitate adjusting your savings and spending. Comprehending the ramifications aids in making knowledgeable choices and modifying your budget correspondingly.

1.3 Remaining Adaptable:

Being adaptable to changes in finances is essential. Be willing to make necessary revisions to your financial objectives, goals, and methods. Being flexible enables you to keep moving forward with your financial goals and adapt well to changing situations.

2. Modifying Budgetary Objectives

2.1 Reevaluating Objectives:
Make sure your financial objectives are still relevant and attainable by regularly reviewing them. A change in your financial status could mean modifying your objectives. For instance, you might think about changing your investing or savings goals if your income rises.

2.2 Creating New Objectives:
Set updated financial goals based on any significant changes to your situation. Set both short- and long-term objectives that correspond to your present priorities and ambitions. During times of transition, setting new goals gives you focus and drive.

2.3 Setting Goal Priorities:
Sort your financial objectives according to priority and urgency. Decide which objectives may be pursued in the

near future and which ones need to be addressed right now. Setting priorities enables you to manage your resources wisely and maintain focus on the important things.

3. Modifying Loan Schedules

3.1 Updates to the Budgets:
Modify your budget to account for variations in your earnings, outlays, and financial objectives. Review your debt payback plans, savings contributions, and spending patterns. A refreshed budget guarantees that, even in times of change, you stay on course and handle your money wisely.

3.2 Adapting Investing Methods:
Based on your updated risk tolerance and financial goals, update your investing plans. Your asset allocation, investment strategy, or retirement planning may need to be adjusted in response to changes in your financial circumstances. To make well-informed judgements, seek advice from a financial counsellor if necessary.

3.3 Modifying Debt Administration:

Review your debt management strategy in the wake of any modifications. You might need to modify your debt repayment plan if your income drops or your expenses rise. To properly manage your commitments, look into options for term negotiations, debt consolidation, or setting high-interest debt as a priority.

4. Enhancing Interaction

4.1 Conversation Open:

Keep lines of communication open on any changes or adjustments to your finances with your partner. Talk about the effects of changes on your plans, aspirations, and financial condition. An open line of communication ensures that both parties are taking the same approach and promotes understanding and collaboration.

4.2 Frequent Visits:

Plan frequent check-ins to assess your plans, goals, and financial situation. During these sessions, talk about any modifications, evaluate your progress, and make any required corrections. Keeping both spouses updated about your financial journey and engaged requires regular check-ins.

4.3 Teamwork in Making Decisions:
Include both spouses in the decision-making process when it comes to monetary adjustments. In order to discover answers that both parties can agree on, collaborative decision-making makes sure that both points of view are taken into account. Additionally, it fortifies the sense of cooperation and shared accountability.

5. Establishing Sturdiness

5.1 Creating Backup Plans:
Make backup plans in case you run into financial difficulties. List potential outcomes, such as losing your job or incurring unforeseen costs, and provide coping mechanisms for each. Having a strategy improves your flexibility and responsiveness.

5.2 Adopting A Financial Literate Mindset:

Develop your financial literacy to be able to handle changes and make wise choices. Keep up with market developments, investment opportunities, and financial trends. You can remain financially stable and adjust to new circumstances by continuing your education.

5.3 Keeping an Upbeat Attitude:

Adopt an optimistic outlook when addressing financial adjustments. Accept the chance to grow and learn from fresh experiences. In times of transition, keeping a positive outlook aids in stress management and motivation maintenance.

6. Seeking Expert Advice

6.1 Financial Advisors Who Consult:

When faced with major financial changes, get professional guidance from financial advisors. Advisors may guide you through challenging financial issues, offer insightful advice, and suggest tactics. Having expert advice guarantees that you stay on course and make wise judgements.

6.2 Making Use of Resources:
Effective change management requires the use of tools, software, and financial resources. You can monitor your progress, make changes, and maintain organisation during periods of transition with the use of financial planning tools, investing platforms, and budgeting apps.

6.3 Investigating Support Networks: Seek guidance and encouragement from support networks, such as online communities or financial support groups. Making connections with people who have experienced comparable difficulties might offer further guidance and support during transitional periods.

7. Honouring Adjustments

7.1 Acknowledging Success:
Honour accomplishments and effective adjustments made at times of transition. Acknowledge the work and

advancement you've done in modifying your financial plan. Honouring accomplishments encourages continued success by reinforcing favourable behaviours.

7.2 Examining Development:

Consider the development and knowledge gained during the adoption process. Think about the ways in which managing transitions has improved your partnership and financial literacy. Accept the trip as a chance for both financial and personal growth.

7.3 Establishing Novel Benchmarks:

Based on your revised financial condition and intentions, set new benchmarks and objectives. Make the most of these achievements to keep moving forward and become financially successful. Establishing new goals helps you stay motivated and focused while you adjust to changing conditions.

Achieving and preserving financial independence as a partnership requires constant adaptation and evolution. A few essential tactics for managing financial transitions are embracing change, updating plans, reevaluating goals, and enhancing communication. Developing resilience, getting expert advice, and appreciating adjustments are all necessary for a happy and prosperous financial path. Couples can thrive financially, accomplish their objectives, and fortify their financial partnership by embracing change with adaptability and cooperation.

Conclusion

As a pair, achieving financial independence is a complex and dynamic process that calls for commitment, thoughtful preparation, and communication. Through strong foundation building and unavoidable change management, Financial Independence for Couples: Building Wealth Together seeks to walk you through the challenges of managing finances as a partnership. As this investigation comes to an end, it's critical to consider the most important lessons learnt and to reaffirm our commitment to reaching our common financial objectives.

- **Key Concepts Recap**

The notion that achieving financial success requires teamwork is fundamental to couples' financial freedom. The first steps include laying a solid foundation by figuring out a common goal and knowing each partner's financial history. Maintaining financial goals and open lines of communication are essential to making sure that both partners are working towards the same goals.

Combining money offers a number of choices, each with pros and cons of its own. While combining finances can make goal-setting and budgeting easier, not every couple will find this to be to their taste. For efficient financial administration, defining financial roles and duties and establishing a shared budget are crucial.

Together, we may build wealth through careful saving, strategic investing, and goal-setting for significant financial objectives. The risk tolerance and financial goals of both partners should be taken into account when designing an effective investing strategy. Teamwork in budgeting and saving improves financial discipline and creates a feeling of purpose. Major life objectives like home ownership or college savings demand careful planning, dedication, and organisation.

Another important component is managing debt, where it's crucial to have plans for consolidating debt and avoiding taking on additional loans. By creating and keeping an emergency fund, you may make sure you're ready for unforeseen costs and financial difficulties. Financial resources are maximised through tax planning and optimisation, which includes choosing to file taxes jointly or separately and making tax-efficient investments.

Financial difficulties will inevitably arise, but maintaining financial harmony can be aided by planning for significant life events and handling conflicts in a constructive manner. A key element of effective money management is keeping lines of communication open and seeking professional counsel.

- **Promoting Ongoing Enhancement**

Being financially independent is a journey rather than a destination. Couples must constantly review and modify their financial plans when their circumstances change, whether as a result of changing jobs, growing families, or unstable economic situations. Long-term performance is influenced by reviewing financial objectives on a regular basis, making necessary budget adjustments, and keeping up with market changes and opportunities.

Celebrating financial achievements encourages continuous development and reinforces beneficial behaviours, such as paying off a sizable debt or hitting a savings goal. Recognising and appreciating the efforts and accomplishments along the route is crucial since these benchmarks demonstrate the dedication and cooperation that propel financial success.

- **Concluding Remarks on Collaborating to Create Wealth**

A shared vision, respect for one another, and a dedication to cooperating to achieve shared objectives are all necessary for a marriage to achieve financial independence. Open communication, group decision-making, and a readiness to adjust to change all improve the process. Financial success is about building a safe and happy future with your partner, not just about amassing cash.

The book's guiding principles offer a road map for couples trying to negotiate the challenges of shared financial management. Couples can attain greater financial independence and stability by learning about each other's financial histories, developing a single financial plan, and adapting to changing conditions over time.

In the end, achieving financial freedom requires cooperation and a common goal. It calls for endurance, adaptability, and a dedication to ongoing development. Adopting these values will improve your relationship and lay a strong basis for a happy future in addition to assisting you in reaching your financial objectives.

Financial Independence for Couples: Building Wealth Together is a source of inspiration as well as guidance. Remember that every couple has a different path to financial freedom, and that your own objectives and values determine what success looks like. As you set out on or keep up your financial independence journey. Together, let's embrace the obstacles, recognise the victories, and relish the process of creating a stable and happy existence.

➢ The Path to Financial Self-Sufficiency

Achieving financial independence is a potent and transformative objective that holds the promise of stability, freedom, and a future moulded by decision rather than accident. This path requires couples to negotiate a challenging terrain of budgeting, cooperation, and decision-making. This chapter explores the necessary actions, typical problems, and methods for creating a solid and prosperous future together as you embark on the path to financial independence.

- **Comprehending Financial Autonomy**

Having enough personal wealth to live well without actively seeking employment is referred to as financial independence. For many, this entails having sufficient investments and assets to meet living expenses and reach long-term financial objectives without the need for conventional work or outside funding. It's a big step forward that gives people the ability to choose what they want instead of what's necessary.

The path to financial freedom for couples starts with a shared vision and a dedication to collaborating towards shared financial goals. This entails coordinating personal objectives with the couple's overall goals, putting together a sound financial strategy, and making wise choices that lead to long-term prosperity.

- **Determining a Common Goal**

A common vision is the first step towards attaining financial freedom as a partnership. This entails talking about and establishing your priorities, values, and financial goals. In order to ensure that both parties are working towards the same goals, a clear and mutually agreed-upon vision helps to build motivation and togetherness.

1. Assign Common Objectives: Talk on what financial independence means to you both to start. Establish both short- and long-term objectives, such as supporting schooling, travelling, buying a property, or retiring early. Set these objectives in order of importance and create a schedule for completion.

2. Set Priorities and Values in Alignment: It's essential to comprehend the priorities and values of each partner. For instance, one couple might put more emphasis on retirement savings than the other, with the former choosing to invest in experiences. When these priorities are in line, a unified plan that represents the goals of both parties can be created.

3. Create a Vision Statement: Formulate a vision statement that summarises your mutual values and financial objectives. This declaration acts as a beacon of guidance, inspiring both parties to overcome obstacles and stay committed to their goals.

- **Creating a Financial Plan**

Creating a thorough financial strategy comes next when you have a common vision. This plan includes specific methods for managing debt, investing, saving, and budgeting. It acts as a road map for reaching your objectives.

1. Establish a Joint Budget: Creating a shared budget is crucial for monitoring earnings, outlays, and saves. Sort spending into categories, establish spending caps, and designate money for investments and savings. A well-organised budget makes it more likely that both partners will be working towards the same financial objectives.

2. Establish an Emergencies Fund: One essential element of financial stability is an emergency reserve. Try to save up three to six months' worth of living expenses in case of unforeseen circumstances like job loss, serious illness, or expensive repairs. Having this safety net in place offers security and lessens financial stress.

3. Construct an Investment Plan: To accumulate wealth and become financially independent, investing is essential. Examine a variety of investing opportunities, including real estate, mutual funds, stocks, and bonds. Choose an investing plan that fits your time horizon, financial objectives, and risk tolerance.

4. Plan for Retirement: Retirement planning entails figuring out how much you must invest and save in order to live comfortably in retirement. Take into account variables including your lifestyle, income sources, and anticipated retirement age. Employ retirement plans like pensions, IRAs, and 401(k)s to accumulate a sizable retirement savings.

- **Managing Typical Difficulties**

There are obstacles in the way of achieving financial freedom. Obstacles that couples may encounter include divergent financial practices, unforeseen costs, and recessions. By proactively addressing these issues, the journey is kept on course and financial stability is preserved.

1. Handling Conflicts Regarding Money: Disagreements may arise from disparities in priorities and spending habits. The secret to overcoming disputes is honest and open communication. Talk about your worries, hear each other out, and collaborate to come up with a solution that works for everyone.

2. Managing Unexpected Expenses: Unexpected costs, including auto repairs or medical bills, can affect your budget. Make sure your emergency fund and budget are flexible enough to handle these costs without causing you to lose track of your long-term objectives.

3. Adapting to Economic Changes: The state of the economy might have an impact on your financial circumstances. Keep up with market developments and make any necessary adjustments to your financial plan. This could entail reevaluating your objectives, changing your investment strategy, or updating your budget.

- **Successful Strategies**

Financial independence demands dedication, self-control, and persistent work. By putting these techniques into practice, you can stay on track and accomplish your objectives.

1. Continually Monitor Progress: Make sure you are on track to meet your goals by keeping a close eye on your financial progress. Periodically review your investments, savings, and budget, and make any necessary modifications.

2. Celebrate Milestones: Mark and commemorate significant junctures along the journey. Reaching financial goals, accumulating more money, or paying off debt are all examples of accomplishments that should be celebrated since they encourage positive behaviour and further advancement.

3. Seek Professional Advice: To obtain knowledgeable views and direction, think about speaking with financial advisors or other specialists. Financial advisors may assist you in creating customised plans, navigating difficult choices, and making the most out of your finances.

4. Encourage Honest Communication: Continue to communicate honestly and openly about money-related issues. Talk about your financial objectives, developments, and worries on a regular basis. Good communication makes it easier to make sure that both parties are on the same page and collaborating to achieve common goals.

As a partnership, achieving financial independence is a fulfilling endeavour that calls for cooperation, dedication, and thoughtful planning. A safe and prosperous future can be built by couples by establishing a shared goal, creating a thorough financial plan, and taking proactive measures to resolve obstacles. Accept the process, don't lose sight of your objectives, and acknowledge and appreciate your progress. Achieving financial freedom involves more than just getting rich; it also entails working together to build a happy and powerful life.

www.ingramcontent.com/pod-product-compliance
Lightning Source LLC
Chambersburg PA
CBHW071912210526
45479CB00002B/381